This book is poignant, insightful and hopeful. It will equip and edify in equal measure.

SAM ALLBERRY
Immanuel Church Nashville; author, *What God Has To Say About Our Bodies*

Why friendship has been diluted and devalued in modern society is a complex question, but the fact of this is incontestable. Karen Martin has written a glorious antidote to this trend, a testimony of a remarkable friendship that spanned generations and life circumstances. Yet I couldn't help thinking as I read that what Karen and Kathleen experienced was a gift from God to them both but also to all who can eavesdrop through Karen's account. This expresses an ideal for friendship that we should all aspire to, a quality of mutual trust and dependence that really ought characterise all kingdom relationships. Along the way, however, this prompts a profound meditation on memory and personhood, human identity and Christian discipleship. I'm delighted to see that this book has finally made it into print.

MARK MEYNELL
Director (Europe & Caribbean), Langham Preaching

Are we more than our memories? Karen Martin shares her journey to focus on a person, not a disease; a loved one living with memory loss, not a dementia victim; and a friend's present and future, not just her fading memories. Walk with an English teacher committed to help an older Christian teacher-friend retain personhood through Dementia by understanding what her friend feels and desires. This book will be a fount of wisdom for anyone who cares for a friend with Dementia.

DAVE DEUEL
Senior Research Fellow, the International Disability Center;
Catalyst for Disability Concerns, the Lausanne Movement;
co-author, *Disability in Mission: The Church's Hidden Treasure.*

T0017892

MEMORABLE LOSS

A story of friendship in the face of dementia

Karen Martin

CHRISTIAN
FOCUS

Copyright © Karen Martin 2023

paperback ISBN 978-1-5271-1002-1
ebook ISBN 978-1-5271-1056-4

10 9 8 7 6 5 4 3 2 1

Published in 2023
by
Christian Focus Publications Ltd,
Geanies House, Fearn, Ross-shire,
IV20 1TW, Great Britain.

www.christianfocus.com

Cover design by
Celia Wood

Printed and bound by
Bell & Bain, Glasgow

Contents

1 The Beginning of the End 11

2 Breaking Taboos 15

3 In the Beginning 23

4 Diagnosis 33

5 A Spoonful of Sugar 45

6 Personal Histories, Changing Times 53

7 Alarm Bells 61

8 Consenting to Move 73

9 Groundhog Day 81

10 Moving On 91

11 In the Margins 101

12 A New Rhythm 107

13 Christmas Selves 115

14 Through a Glass Darkly 125

15 A Sense of Place 131

16 Shifting Sands 139

17 Abiding Narratives 147

18 Language of Consent 155

19 The Narrowing Gate 163

20 Holding On 171

21 A Gift 177

22 Complications of Consent 183

23 Tomorrow 191

24 The End 195

25 Not the End 201

Acknowledgements 205

Bibliographic References 207

For Kathleen, with much love
And for Bri, Emily and James
who always believed in this book

Author's Note

All the medical and legal information contained in *Memorable Loss* is asserted as correct at date of writing.

This is a true story, but for the purposes of privacy, some names have been changed in accordance with the wishes of friends and sources.

In order to preserve the anonymity of staff and current residents, I have renamed the care home, Bluebell House. It remains the best example of care I have ever seen, and I will always be indebted to all who work there, for their good care of my friend.

1
The Beginning of the End

Fireworks lit up a sky already opaque with smoke. Children darted free from their parents, hiding behind benches, small hands covering their ears. Still, they dared to peep out, squealing as the dark night filled with explosions of red, white and green. Kathleen snuggled closer to me in the November dankness, the bear-like fur of her big Russian hat tickling my face. She chuckled at the antics of the children, exclaiming at the noise. Her hearing aids were safely tucked away in my pocket, a small act of insurance that the display wouldn't prove too overwhelming. Our bench was furthest from the pyrotechnics – previous experience had shown me that being close to the parapet that overlooked the garden was far too close for comfort. From this vantage point, we watched other residents and their families make the same discovery. Wheelchairs were pulled hastily back, and those who were able, took a few steps nearer the house.

This was our fifth bonfire night at Bluebell House, and it would be our last. Nothing about that evening marked it out as seminal. Nothing about Kathleen suggested anything other than a zest for life. She was not going to stay in the warmth of the lounge to watch the fireworks when she could be outside in the chill autumn air. She may no longer have been able to discern the distinctive smell of cordite released into the atmosphere with each burst of noisy colour, but her eyes could see enough of the magic to relish being amongst it all. Kathleen was part of something, surrounded by people she had grown to love.

I have a grainy photo of that night, snapped by one of the care home staff; an opportune pointing of a mobile phone in our direction, the pixels struggling against the dark and the smoke. There we are captured in the last moment of normality, snuggling her sheepskin coat against my all-weather three-in-one in an attempt to keep warm in the damp November air. She is very much alive and full of joy.

Kathleen was my friend. Not enough is written or spoken about such a bond. Both voluntary and uncomplicated by duty or expectation, there is no weight of history to encumber it. In many ways it is temporal; different people are important at various stages of our lives. Players grace the stage with us for a time and then fade into the wings with no discernible parting.

Kathleen was not such a player. With an age gap of forty-three years, ours was an unusual connection. Though she didn't enter stage-right into my life until I was in my thirties and she was in her seventies, we stuck with each other. Her parting, rather than being part of the usual ebb and flow, left a gaping hole.

We met in a small church group. At first, I saw a slightly formidable woman. She was wise, organised and had an air of unmistakeable authority. A friend of mine still saw Kathleen as her Deputy Head Teacher, reminding her of her schooldays. Over 30 years later, she still straightened her back and confessed to a twinge of fear when their paths crossed. Kathleen retired the year I began studying for my O Levels, and it was her genuine interest in my job as an English teacher that forged the initial link in our friendship. In this small church group, I was able to speak openly about the dual pressures of full-time work and bringing up a young family. Like many people, I was reasonably adept at juggling the various demands, but it was exhausting, and causing me to question my priorities. Everyone at that group was supportive and kind, but Kathleen really understood.

I started giving her a lift to the weekly meetings after she admitted that she no longer enjoyed driving in the dark. I lived nearby, so it was the logical, practical solution. Those short trips marked the beginning of a deeper friendship where I learnt about Terence, her brother – they looked like twins apparently – and her nephews Philip and Matthew. I learnt that she had never had a romantic relationship, instead willingly dedicating her life first to education and later to charitable works. She trusted God's plans for her life, and never doubted them. She lived responsibly, sensibly and completely independently. Kathleen never wanted to be a burden on anyone else. She had saved money for the future.

Through these car journeys, I also realised she was lonely. Kathleen had not had a family Christmas for years. In a decision taken decades before, she had decided to give her brother the undiluted joy of his own children and grandchildren – *he didn't need to feel responsible for his spinster sister*, she said – so Christmas Day was spent volunteering at a local lunch for the elderly. Already beyond her three-score-years and ten, I managed to persuade her that she had done her duty and that we would love her to join our festive celebrations. We had food, merriment and room to spare.

Without a script, Kathleen moved to centre stage. Our friendship tilted to something more intimate, more like family.

That was nearly twenty years ago. She became such a fixture in our lives that my children, now adults themselves, can barely remember a time when she wasn't there.

It might seem alien to some that we were convinced our friendship was God-given. We both believed that there was a plan in our meeting and developing a bond that defied the age gap. Neither of us was unhappy or needy – neither of us was looking for the other – but there was guidance and growth in our relationship that led to a purpose and privilege that neither of us could have foreseen.

We couldn't have known as we pulled crackers around my table that first shared Christmas that it would be me who sat with Kathleen during diagnostic tests for Alzheimer's, who tried to help her reinterpret a world she had spent her career interpreting for others. We couldn't have known it would be me who would need to learn to advocate for her in a society that, whilst acknowledging there is increasing prevalence of dementia, is not yet adept at accommodating it.

Dementia is experienced in different forms, in different ways and is coped with differently by different people. But, despite the life-changing effects of Alzheimer's, this story is overwhelmingly one of love and persistence. It is about remembering that whatever the disease does, whatever detriments it inflicts, the heart of a person remains steadfast.

Kathleen knew I was writing this. It began as a polemic urging societal change, but has morphed into something quite different. I hope she would be proud to be held in these pages as testimony to our bond, but I also think she would see the bigger picture. We may have been players on our particular stage, but it is a storyline that is enacted in countless families across the globe. It is a story that needs to be told, allowing friendship rather than the disease to hold the narrative thrust. Ours is a story where Alzheimer's created a stronger bond, where ordinary friendship grew through the challenges of dementia. This – I like to think she would be nodding sagely – is a more effective way to grow change.

Watching the fireworks and seeing Kathleen's joy in the colours that blazed in the sky, I was certain of who she was.

2
Breaking Taboos

Kathleen knew she might be facing a future with Alzheimer's before I was ready to accept the collection of symptoms that were becoming increasingly apparent. A dementia diagnosis was too big, too fearful for me to contemplate. I found it easier to rationalise things by blaming her gaps in memory on simple old age. Surely everyone forgets things?

No one is certain what causes Alzheimer's, but many live with its devastating effects. Whilst the Alzheimer's Society estimates there are about 850,000 diagnosed cases in the UK, many more people are affected by the detriments associated with the disease.[1] For every person with dementia, there are implications of care and impacts on relationships. It is a disease that steals into families with consequences for everyone. For Kathleen, it meant surrendering her independence, little bit by little bit. For Terence, Philip and Matthew it meant learning to trust me, eventually allowing me to become, as Philip termed it, *the eyes and ears of the family.*

It's hard to know where it starts, because forgetfulness is usually the siren call to medicalisation. And it is true that, as we age, we all have an increased tendency to forget. Our processing skills slow, but it is the forgetting that makes us aware of a deficit. The term dementia refers to global cognitive impairment, but the common

---

1. Allzheimer's Society, 'Facts for the Media.'

ground is memory loss.[2] I don't know what Kathleen noticed first, what caused her to start questioning her own cognition, eventually pushing her to be brave enough to admit there might be a problem. I'm not sure what she was finding hard to deal with when she was on her own because I was looking at Kathleen and not seeing anything amiss.

I didn't see because I did not want to see. This was more than wilful individual blindness; it was born from deep ideological assumptions. Brought up in the Thatcher era that shouted we could all be what we wanted to be, I am a product of an increasingly individualised culture. We are taught to prize intelligence and autonomy above all else. Dementia takes autonomy away. It is not something we are readily equipped for.

I had been drenched in the concept of modern identity. Stephen King, in his book *Duma Key*, asserts that our identity is rooted in what we remember.[3] This resounds with contemporary thought that memory is wholly fundamental to who we are. Author Carlos Ruiz Zafón is uncompromising in his view that, 'we are what we remember, and the less we remember, the less we are.'[4] Such dependence on memory as self is understandable – we gain empathy and wisdom from experience, and in order to apply these we need to be able to access the past. Our memories give us a sense of connection to people, places and things; they help us to continually construct who we are. Memories validate our experiences.

But they are not the only way. Human character is not simply constructed from recall – babies are born with personalities, and even twins whose childhood experience is the most directly comparable, have individual, separating personality traits. The persistence in modern thinking that it is only memory that forms and shapes us risks dehumanising those who live with Alzheimer's and other dementia and memory disorders. This persistence in modern thinking ensures that dementia remains taboo.

My friendship with Kathleen has made me question society's seeming dismissal of those with memory impairment. A former deputy head of a large girls' school, Kathleen had once commanded an audience with ease – she earned the nickname 'the look' because

---

2. Waldemar and Burns, *Alzheimer's Disease*, Ch 1:1.

3. King, *Duma Key*, 442.

4. Cruz, 'Author Carlos Ruiz Zafón.'

her penetrating gaze was sufficient to silence a hall full of girls. Once diagnosed with Alzheimer's disease her confidence quickly eroded as she became fearful that by forgetting a name or losing the thread of a conversation, she would publicly embarrass herself. It became easier to stay away, to cancel social dates. It was easier to hide than face the collective awkwardness of a society whose default setting is autonomy.

We do not have many answers – the brain is not fully understood, and there is, so far, no cure for Alzheimer's – but Kathleen showed me that we are so much more than the sum total of what we remember. There is deepening trust in deepening dependence. Perhaps dementia can help us to rewrite the cultural history that sets individualism and independence at its heart.

As early as 350bce Aristotle wrote an essay noting that it is the very young and very old who are defective in memory. His explanation was that both are in a state of flux – the young are developing and the old are decaying.[5] And whilst we don't like to accept the notion of decay, that is exactly what is happening to the Alzheimer's brain. Whilst we can acknowledge the facts surrounding cell death and brain atrophy as we age, it is not a given that we should also accept that detriments in memory function naturally equate to being less than we were.

Kathleen may have lost significant short-term memory – even her initial diagnostic tests revealed this – but her personality remained present. Facts, places and people were lost but her character, her essence, was not.

On one level, it is easy to accept that we deteriorate as we get older. Researchers at the Massachusetts Institute of Technology have noted that our raw speed in processing information peaks as early as eighteen years of age, and then immediately begins to decline. Our short-term memory continues to improve until twenty-five where it plateaus for about a decade before the downturn occurs. With regard to emotional intelligence, however, the peak occurs much later. It is not until our forties or fifties that ability to empathise reaches its height.[6] Perhaps it is this fortunate serendipity that meant I was able to reach beyond Alzheimer's and hold fast to our friendship. But, whatever our emotional intelligence, we cannot escape the fact that

---

5. Bloch, *Aristotle on Memory and Recollection*.

6. MIT News, 'The Rise and Fall of Cognitive Skills,' 1.

from as young as twenty, we begin to lose neurons to the ageing process, and, by the age of seventy-five, we all have 10 per cent fewer than at our optimum cognition.[7] The adult brain declines in volume by about 5 per cent per decade from the age of forty, and it is thought that deterioration in capacity accelerates from the seventh decade.[8]

But it is heartening that Aristotle chose to include a qualifier in his assessment of memory loss – the *very* old and the *very* young; one thing modern researchers agree on is that the single largest risk-factor for development of dementia is age.[9] And it is the very old who are at most risk. One recent study estimated that between the ages of sixty-five and sixty-nine just 2 per cent of the world population has significant cognitive deficit, but between eighty-five and eighty-nine years old the percentage diagnosed with some form of dementia goes up to 18 per cent, reaching 41 per cent for those aged between eighty-nine and ninety-five.[10] So, whilst the word *epidemic* has been bandied about in the popular press with regard to the prevalence of Alzheimer's in the modern world, it could be that with improvements in our knowledge of nutrition, the benefits of exercise and the developments in modern medicine, more of us are simply living longer.

This algorithm works for Kathleen. She only began admitting symptoms of memory loss and confusion in her eighty-fourth year. Many of us now expect to live into our ninth decade, and our children are expected to exceed even that. As yet, no breakthrough treatments have been found that reverse the process of memory loss. Indeed, memory and its mechanisms remained an intractable mystery to medical science until the pioneering, and some would say, vainglorious surgery undertaken in asylums in the United States throughout the 1940s and 1950s.

William Beecher Scoville established the Department of Neurosurgery in Hartfield Hospital, Connecticut in 1939. Working with asylum patients, he found that post-operative effects of the lobotomies he performed not only pacified restless patients, but in cases where epilepsy was a further complicating factor to mental

---

7. Indiana Public Media, 'What Happens When You Lose Neurons? | A Moment of Science.'

8. Peters, 'Ageing and the Brain,' 84.

9. Nilsson and Ohta, *Dementia and Memory*, 8.

10. Taylor, *The Fragile Brain*, 92.

illness, the surgery also provided respite from seizures. This prompted his proposal to perform psychosurgery on twenty-seven-year-old Henry Molaison, a young man whose quality of life was seriously impaired by frequent grand and petit mal seizures. The key difference in this patient was that he had no evidence of any other cognitive impairment or mental health disorder.

At a neurophysiological symposium in Hollywood, Florida on 23 April 1953, Scoville concurred with Yale researchers that little was comprehensively known about the brain's limbic system – the area we associate with motivation, emotion, learning and memory. He described his findings as 'small bits of passing data' accumulated through the experience of operating on over two hundred patients.[11] The operations in question, known as uncotomies, were procedures where a small section of the limbic system – the uncus, situated deep in the brain – was deliberately cut to treat those suffering from repeated psychosis. A medial temporal lobotomy was a development of this operation and involved creating lesions throughout the limbic region of the brain. Admitting that one of his psychotic patients had experienced amnesic tendencies after the operation, Scoville publicly acknowledged that the function of the hippocampal region, a key part of the limbic system, remained largely unknown.[12]

With the operation on Henry Molaison in August of 1953, the mystery was tragically solved. The hippocampal region was the undeniable seat of memory in the brain. Unable to form any new memories from the date of the surgery, Henry Molaison would never again live independently. His working memory was very short – if a researcher he had been working with happened to leave the room and return, he had no capacity to recall anything about the person or their relationship to him. Any memory of his past life pre-dated the operation. He was unable to navigate around the hospital or even his parents' home, and therefore something as simple as a trip to once familiar shops became impossible.

With patient H.M., as he was known until his death in 2002, doctors and researchers were able to learn much about how we form memory. What we still don't know, however, is what causes it to decline. Beyond Aristotelian old age, there have been many theories regarding genes, proteins, and neurofibrillary tangles,

11. Dittrich, *Patient H.M.*, 206.
12. Dittrich, *Patient H.M.*, 206.

known as taus. Many of these have credence, but research in each remains ongoing.

Modern ideology surrounding memory – that we are what we remember – even pervades discussion of neurosurgery, psychology and dementia. In his book about his grandfather's surgery on Molaison, Luke Dittrich writes, 'Memories make us: everything we are is everything we were.'[13]

We associate Alzheimer's primarily with memory loss. This is, however, only one indicator of the disease. Loss of confidence and increased anxiety are also common markers. Kathleen became aware that she could no longer cope as well as she had done. She asked for reassurance over simple, everyday tasks, such as compiling a shopping list or doing the washing. She became increasingly anxious when we were out, letting me take the lead in conversations if we met someone she knew. It seemed like she was beginning to lose touch with who she had once been – the confidence and authority that marked her out as capable and dependable were ebbing away – arguably, she was losing her former identity. When shown photographs of a world trip she had made post-retirement, she responded to them with sadness; *'I don't know how I managed to do all that on my own. I certainly couldn't now.'* Alzheimer's disease made Kathleen feel less than she had been – such awareness of confusion and reduction of capability in the face of societal expectation for autonomy, can quickly lead to a loss of sense of self.

Dementia is a disease of brain atrophy, involving the gradual destruction of synapses – the junctions between nerve cells where electrical impulses pass; axons – the threadlike part of nerve cells responsible for conducting the impulses; and finally the cells themselves.[14] Different abilities are lost at different rates. To map Alzheimer's broadly in terms of memory, we first notice a decline in episodic function – the ability to recall recent events and conversations. Semantic memory – where we store knowledge of language, concepts and facts, outlasts episodic reliability. The final grouping of memory function is implicit or procedural – things like muscle memory, our physical ability to walk, chew and swallow. It is only in the final stages of dementia that loss of these functions is apparent.

---

13. Dittrich, *Patient H.M.*, xiv.
14. Taylor, *The Fragile Brain*, 53.

But if we persist in thinking, as reflected in literature, that 'we are our memory'[15] then it is very difficult to value the older population who are losing theirs. With cases of dementia, validation often has to come from outside. Kathleen Taylor writes with warmth as she explains that people with dementia are 'each unique, each with a valuable life history and identity. That identity may seem to slip away as the disease takes hold, but how much of that is in the mind of the onlooker?'[16]

This presents us with a significant challenge. Taylor seems to be throwing down the gauntlet that challenges us to look beyond ideology, beyond what culture has taught us to prize. In her studies, she has seen something more persistent than memory. And other scientific studies have also corroborated that those living with dementia feel as they have always done.[17] They may be confused at times, they may be anxious but, at a core level, an emotional one, they are who they have always been. The smile I see radiating from photographs of my friend Kathleen from her graduation at the age of twenty-two to her care home chair on her ninety-first birthday just weeks from her death, show her essence to be the same as it had always been. She could no longer remember much at all, but she knew when she was with people who loved her, and her smile expressed a character that had not been lost to the ravages of disease. Perhaps with an increase in dementia worldwide, it is time to break the taboo; it is time for a shift in popular opinion about what makes us who we are.

---

15.   Borges, *In Praise of Darkness.*

16.   Taylor, *The Fragile Brain*, 21.

17.   Karger, 'Emotional Experience in Patients with Advanced Alzheimer's Disease from the Perspective of Families, Professional Caregivers, Physicians, and Scientists.'

3
In the Beginning

Compensation and Collusion

Kathleen was my mentor and confidante. Sharing a dry sense of humour, we kept each other amused. We often pondered how two completely unrelated people could be so similar – and not only in personality. She was tall, wore glasses and had silvered hair. All those features could be used to describe me, and we were frequently mistaken for mother and daughter. She liked to refer to me as the sister she never had, and I regularly objected to that on the basis of the nearly half-century which separated us!

Neither of us was sentimental. Pragmatism and practicality defined us both. You were unlikely to find either one of us weeping at a film or crying tears of frustration. Solution-finders rather than shoulders to cry on, perhaps we were both regarded as formidable in the classroom; certainly neither of us was overly troubled by discipline issues in our careers. But there was a core of kindness running through Kathleen, and I hope I have something of that in me too. We cared about the education of our students, and we cared as much about their wellbeing as their exam results.

I have often joked that 'she was sensible' might be my epitaph. It could certainly form a part of Kathleen's. There is also a strong

23

sense of duty that runs through me. I feel that I was born with it. Potentially an ugly word that only says *should*, it is also an undervalued word. In my heart, it forms a compulsion to care. It goes beyond what I *should* do to what I *could* do. In this subtle difference resides a completely different definition of duty. An only child, I always knew I wanted to be there for my own parents as they aged, and I hope I will be. Kathleen shared this trait too. She had looked after her mother and made sure that post-retirement she remained useful to others, looking always at what she *could* do.

So when I looked at Kathleen in the spring light of an April morning and noticed something different about her, it is not surprising that I sought a practical solution. I remember what prompted it – one of those seemingly insignificant moments that become etched on the memory like a cinema reel. It was an ordinary Sunday morning. It was sunny, and I was drinking coffee with a friend after the morning church service. As I looked up, I spotted Kathleen across the church hall. She was nursing a brown, Pyrex coffee cup in her hands – strong, little milk and two sugars – Kathleen would take no notice of dietary advice to reduce caffeine and sugar intake, 'I walk every day,' was her oft-quoted cure-all. Her hair was lacquered, and her lips sported her signature shade of pink, just a tad brighter than was entirely necessary. She had on her Sunday best – a good suit whose skirt fell to her shins and the jacket, short-sleeved and done up over a white cotton blouse typifying Kathleen's smart, respectable, ex-schoolteacher style.

Glancing over at her, caught in the light from the full-height windows, I felt a creeping certainty that something was not quite right.

Kathleen stood head and shoulders above most people in the room, her presence reminiscent of the authority she had wielded at work. She was slim, though her wardrobe testified to a mindset that wasn't convinced of this. Her clothes ranged from size fourteen to eighteen, despite the fact that, since I had known her, she had never been more than a twelve. As I replay that morning in the busy hall, filled with people, it is silent – my memory has muted everyone else, rendering them out of focus – it is the defining moment when I saw Kathleen with new eyes. I realised that she was no longer slender, but thin. Her pale green suit hung from her and I suspected a safety pin was drawing the waistband together. It seemed incomprehensible. I hadn't spotted it the previous week when I had taken Kathleen out. I hadn't spotted it when a group of us had been away for the weekend. Something was going on.

I turned to my friend, 'Do you think Kathleen is alright? She's looking a bit thin.'

Glancing over at her ex-deputy head, she reassured me. Something about the fact that Kathleen had taught so many of our congregation meant lots of people never stopped seeing her as the efficient, slightly brusque, capable teacher. I knew about presenting a public face and pretending an authority that at times we might not feel. My friend saw Kathleen chatting confidently and doing what she had always done. She didn't think she was especially thin. She was fine.

But she wasn't. She was already at the mercy of Alzheimer's disease, though it would be some time before we recognised it for what it was. Her thinness was a symptom of memory loss – before any other signs or concerns surfaced, Kathleen had been forgetting to eat. Alzheimer's was inching its way through her brain cells and tricking her. I know now that if she looked at her watch and it was past one o'clock, she simply assumed that she had eaten lunch. Of course she had. Why wouldn't she? A creature of routine, dictated by her watch rather than her stomach, she was inadvertently missing several meals a week. Though still outwardly fine and active, the disease was beginning to do its work.

I didn't see Alzheimer's that day – it didn't even cross my mind. All I saw was evidence that age seemed to be catching up with Kathleen. I resolved to visit her more often and see if she would appreciate a hand with shopping and cooking.

It is common for the early signs and symptoms of dementia to be overlooked. In retrospect, we can often see changes in behaviour that should have been red flags for early diagnosis, but it is only in hindsight that we see them so clearly. A friend told me that her mum stopped baking flapjacks for the grandchildren. Like Kathleen's thinness, this was explained away as a sign of advancing years. No medical textbook cites lack of baking as a symptom of dementia, but, in this case, it was out of character. She had always baked her welcome.

Looking back, I can see things that may have been evidence of the neurological changes taking place in Kathleen's brain. In the months before diagnosis, she informed me that her washing machine, vacuum cleaner and portable television needed replacing. I had no cause to question her, and, after checking with the family to make sure they were happy for me to help her spend large sums of money, I merely accompanied her to the department store, helping Kathleen to select new models in a given price range. That so many electrical items would fail in such a short space of time now seems incredible; it was far more likely that she had got confused when trying to use them and made an assumption about their obsolescence.

Hindsight makes it clear that I missed things that signified a cognitive shift. Her family hadn't questioned it either. We were all rooted in her autonomy and capability.

Familiarity, however, is not necessarily any real help in identifying the signs of the disease. Studies have shown that the pathology of Alzheimer's disease is evident in the brain many years before a clinical diagnosis can be made, and therefore micro changes in behaviour, thinking and emotional responses are likely to have taken place and, crucially, been continually adapted to and accommodated over time.[1] Such adaptation masks the extent of neurological change. We are an adaptable species; we cope well with moving to new locations, learning new languages, adopting new skills and responding to the changing dynamics of personal relationships. And with dementia, biology enables us to compensate to a certain extent – if our brains begin to atrophy, we adapt, and even more readily if we happen to be educated. The current hypothesis is that education creates cognitive reserve – a capacity for the brain to compensate for early deterioration and make new pathways.[2]

In the normal ageing process, it has been seen that everyone compensates to some extent – our memory function in particular becomes increasingly bilateral, rather than relying simply on one side of the brain – but in those with Alzheimer's it seems that the coping mechanisms are even more complex.[3] Crucially, prolonged ability to mask symptoms can be an indicator for sudden, rapid decline. The most likely outcome of those who have significant cognitive reserve is that diagnosis is later and, once Alzheimer's disease pathology emerges, the progress of dementia is more rapid.[4] Famous examples of Iris Murdoch and Terry Pratchett bear this out.

---

1. Mortimer et al., 'Very Early Detection of Alzheimer Neuropathology and the Role of Brain Reserve in Modifying Its Clinical Expression,' 218.

2. Stern, 'Cognitive Reserve in Ageing and Alzheimer's Disease,' 1006.

3. Peters, 'Ageing and the Brain,' 84.

4. Stern, 'Cognitive Reserve in Ageing and Alzheimer's Disease,' 1009.

A typical compensating behaviour is that of avoidance, and it is often one of the presenting symptoms of the initial stages of Alzheimer's. Kathleen cited lack of energy when dropping out of the rota to lead Bible studies and used it again when she declined to come on the annual group holiday. Later, she told me that she was getting too old to come out in the evenings; she wanted her bed, and thus her attendance at the group stopped altogether. These were all very reasonable – Kathleen was by now in her early eighties – nobody questioned her decisions at all.

But loss of social confidence may not be due to advanced years and increased fatigue. They can be markers for depression, isolation or loneliness, but crucially they can also be the initial presentation of the brain atrophy associated with dementia.

Anxiety and lack of confidence are apparent from the very early stages of Alzheimer's disease, and these demons are hard to battle with.[5] After she had excused herself from evening activities, Kathleen began avoiding situations where she might encounter uncertainty. Friends who had regularly driven her to church reported that there was often a series of phone calls, beginning Saturday evening and repeated early Sunday morning to say that she was feeling too poorly, or a little under the weather, or was just too tired to go this week. They asked me, 'Did I know she had been ill? Was everything okay?'

Clearly everything was not okay, but Kathleen was not poorly in the conventional sense of the word. She was withdrawing from a life she had formerly embraced because anticipation of the church service and subsequent socialising were causing profound anxiety – enough to make her feel ill. Even before diagnosis, Alzheimer's was robbing her of an experience she had previously found enriching, even fundamental to her life.

When she did go to church, she could no longer concentrate for the length of a sermon. It was too much information for her brain to hold, and she lost context quickly. In later years when we occasionally attended special services together, I would watch fondly as her eyelids drooped and her head sunk into her chin, before jerking her awake a few seconds later.

Alzheimer's has been a frequent visitor in my family. Perhaps it was this subconscious thread that led me to spend more time with

---

5. Ferretti et al., 'Anxiety and Alzheimer's Disease.'

Kathleen. Not spoken about or acknowledged as much in the 1980s, it was some time before we recognised that my grandmother and her mother before her, suffered from the declines now commonly associated with dementia. Then it was dismissed as senility associated with age, and at diagnosis the label was senile dementia rather than Alzheimer's or other specific dementia types.

We first realised my great-gran, Maude, had the disease when a neighbour rang to report that she had been found wandering the local village in the middle of the night. Likewise, my grandmother's symptoms were not picked up early. My grandfather had colluded to mask many of her idiosyncrasies from the rest of the family, and it was only after his death that we found stockpiles of tinned food way beyond their sell-by dates which she had refused to let go of.

Like my grandfather, most of us work to collude with those we love. We help them to compensate for symptoms by taking over responsibilities that they had once been able to perform for themselves – we hide evidence of irrational behaviour from other people. This reticence is proof of societal taboo stemming from ideology dominant in the Western world, that we are only worthwhile if we are both fully functioning and useful. Fear of memory loss is endemic – the Alzheimer's Society reports that dementia is the most feared health condition in the UK, perhaps explaining also why 62 per cent of people surveyed felt a diagnosis would mean their life was over.[6] Considering the prevalence of literature that conforms with the idea that 'Memories make us. Everything we are is everything we were,'[7] it is unsurprising that when faced with cognitive change our first response is denial, both for ourselves and those we love.

Colluding with those in the early, often pre-diagnosis stages of the disease is therefore a natural, protective response. In doing Kathleen's shopping with her I was ensuring that her fridge was stocked for the week, working with her to negotiate a problem, rather than face it head on.

When it was apparent that she was still losing weight, I began to check her food supplies. Sometimes there were too many meals left for the number of days remaining in the week. We did visit the

---

6. Alzheimer's Society, 'Over Half of People Fear Dementia Diagnosis, 62 per Cent Think It Means "Life Is Over."'

7. Dittrich, *Patient H.M.*, xiv.

doctor, and like so many other people, we said everything was fine; Kathleen was just having difficulty keeping to a healthy weight.

Armed with carrier bags brimming with nutritional shakes, we had a solution. I made sure that I visited her every day and checked that food was being eaten. If there was a main meal left in the fridge which should have formed that day's lunch, I would warm it up for her, serve it and then stay with her while she ate. Kathleen was not, as far as I was able to deduce, aware that I was supervising her. It was just a friendly encounter at the end of the day.

Any fears we harboured of Alzheimer's remained unvoiced. I reported to Philip, her nephew, that we had visited the GP. I told him her blood pressure was fine, and that there were no changes in medication. I told him that I was helping Kathleen with her shopping and encouraging her to drink shakes to supplement her diet. I let him know that I was on hand to take her to the doctors if needed, and that I was now picking up her hearing aid batteries for her and changing them regularly. Nothing was wrong; Kathleen was just getting older and needed a bit of support from a friend.

Then I began to find cuttings from her daily newspaper that Kathleen had circled in blue biro and left on the dining room table. All the articles were on memory loss and Alzheimer's. It was as if she were deliberately leaving them out in places where I would see them so that we might start a conversation. But it was a conversation I wasn't ready for, and one she wasn't brave enough to articulate. She exhibited no significant symptoms. She was great company, chatty; she still walked for her paper and caught the bus to her midweek fellowship group. She was well-groomed and her house was clean and tidy. I just needed to make sure that she ate.

Some of the ways the disease manifested itself were textbook. We would be out and about in town and meet a former colleague or past pupil, and she would have no idea who they were. But still we colluded – all this was explainable – when you teach hundreds of children year on year, you will forget most of them. It is a fact that the students who get stuck in our heads are those who have been spectacularly gifted or spectacularly difficult! I totally empathised and was quick to reassure her that I too had memory blanks as far as names were concerned. I have holes in my head when I fish for a word or try to put a name to a face. Doesn't everyone? How to distinguish the disease from absentmindedness, stress and general decline in old age is not an exact science.

Kathleen wrote everything down. This had always been the case and so it rang no alarm bells for me or for Philip when he came down to visit his aunt that summer. There were to-do lists in the kitchen, birthday lists in the diary and a record of correspondence going back years. Notes of appointments were duplicated by the telephone, on the calendar, in the diary and in the hall. Kathleen was creating a memory system which was physical, visible. She was developing a system which masked her underlying pathology, compensating for cognitive decline. But even as she did so, it was becoming increasingly clear that her need to write things down was bothering her.

She told me what she used to do at school, 'A girl would often just stop me in the corridor. She would have something pressing to tell me, or a question that needed a lengthy answer that I didn't have time to give there and then.'

She paused in her retelling to correct a detail, 'It could be a girl or a member of staff – everyone thought that their request was the most urgent. In every instance I told them to go to my office where they would find a pad – they should write their message down and I would attend to it as soon as I could. Things written down were far less likely to be forgotten.'

At first, I regarded this as just another of her anecdotes, but on reflection I realise that it was her way of expressing concern. Fearful of losing her capacity to remember, she worried that such loss of cognition might somehow have been her fault, have been prevented if she had behaved differently. Later, post-diagnosis, Kathleen would ask me directly whether I thought that such dependence on notes might have caused the dementia.

'Perhaps I should have made more effort,' she said. 'Perhaps I failed to train my memory.'

There is no evidence that being a note-maker in life is linked to poor memory. It is far more likely to be symptomatic of good sense and organisation. Indeed, Kathleen's degree-level education, demanding full-time job over many years, foreign travel, hobbies and interests meant that she did everything she could to maintain her brain health. It has been noted that alongside the benefits of education those who engage in more leisure activities have 38 per cent less risk of developing dementia.[8] Kathleen did everything right. Alzheimer's is not a respecter of effort.

The beginnings of dementia often present in lack of confidence in areas where previously the person has been capable. Becoming quieter, refusing invitations or no longer issuing them can be a sign that something is wrong. In the months before her diagnosis, I had been Kathleen's taxi to regular coffee mornings with a group of ex-colleagues. It was when I picked her up one day that her friend drew me to one side.

'Is Kathleen alright?'

'Yes, I think so. Why?'

'She doesn't join in with the chat very much these days, that's all. She's very quiet and that's unlike her. A few of us have noticed and so we thought I should ask you.'

I didn't think too much of this exchange. Kathleen's hearing aids distorted sounds if she was in a crowded place, especially where multiple conversations were happening at the same time. I reassured her that Kathleen was fine. She managed with little difficulty in a one-to-one conversation and so it was easy to attribute her lack of animation to increased deafness.

Looking back at all the evidence that testifies to Alzheimer's disease, my naivety screams at me. Wilful blindness in the hope that I could protect my friend from a future nobody would ask for. An upstanding member of the local community for over fifty years, Kathleen had taken care to present herself well. She was intelligent, reliable and independent. She never wanted to be a burden on anyone – she told me this time and time again. Aware that her nearest relatives were over a hundred miles away and were fraternal, she didn't want her nephews to feel responsible for her care as she aged. She had taken out insurances against the need for a nursing home; she had saved her pension and invested a portion of her salary for a rainy day. Kathleen was defined by good sense, intelligence and her independence; Alzheimer's, or any admission of its possibility, threatened all of that. I wanted to walk alongside her, protecting her, facilitating her presentation of herself as she had always been. I became a willing accomplice in anything that enabled her to retain dignity and independence.

---

8. Stern, 'Cognitive Reserve in Ageing and Alzheimer's Disease.'

When her turn came to host the retired teachers' tea party, I suggested that I act as baker and waitress. She clapped her hands whilst palpable relief crossed her features. Kathleen was able to enjoy the role of lady-of-the-manor whilst I poured tea and cut slivers of Victoria sponge onto delicate fine-china plates. Neither of us admitted out loud that she couldn't have handled the responsibility on her own.

Other things began to change – Kathleen had always done the crossword in *The Times*, relishing the jumbo version on a Saturday. I would often find the large puzzle next to the telephone in the kitchen – a testament to her weekly phone calls with a friend, when they would chat over the trickier clues and complete the grid together. Increasingly, more and more of the clues would remain unanswered, and by the time Monday's paper was bought, the unfinished giant puzzle would be demoted to the recycling pile.

'We had too much to chat about,' Kathleen would explain, 'we didn't get round to all the clues.'

But then I began to find barely attempted or not-even-opened crosswords on the coffee table. When Kathleen's friend happened to ring while I was there, she took the opportunity to express concern, 'I'm glad to have caught you. You see, she isn't phoning me very often anymore, and she never wants to discuss the crossword. Is everything alright?'

'I'm not sure,' I admitted for the first time, lowering my voice so that Kathleen wouldn't overhear.

This was her best friend, a colleague of decades, someone she had maintained weekly contact with ever since they had both retired. Like me, she was worried, but hadn't wanted to upset Kathleen by inferring something serious might be wrong.

The catalogue of coincidence was becoming too full to ignore. Kathleen had lost confidence, was no longer doing the crossword or proactively phoning her friend. She felt unequal to the task of hosting a coffee morning, and she was quiet in company. Sometimes she opted not to go to social events she had previously relished. Amidst all this, she was still thin. I was policing her shopping and eating, but it wasn't enough.

It was time for me to ring Philip.

4

Diagnosis

The decision to seek medical help when there is the possibility of a dementia diagnosis is emotionally and socially complex. Many are fearful of bringing concerns to the attention of the GP because they don't want to draw attention to a disease that is met with persistent negative connotations.[1] Modern society fears dementia. Perhaps this is because, at some subliminal level, it serves as a stark reminder of mortality – that we are organic beings subject to disease and decay. Or, more intuitively, perhaps fear is the natural reaction to a disease that removes independence as it wages war with our memories. Fearing Kathleen's loss of independence is certainly what prevented me from opening the conversation that we could have had, and maybe should have had, months before we did.

But even healthy memory is selective and reconstructive. We forget more than we remember – holidays blend, evenings spent on the sofa watching TV become cumulative memories rather than a series of specific incidents. Remembering is a fundamental part of being human, but we are not computers and recall is one of the most flawed skills in our arsenal. It is common for most of us to fear Alzheimer's whilst remaining perfectly content in the everyday unreliability involved in the reconstruction of our own narrative. We accept that the passage of time serves to edit and recreate treasured memories. For the most part, we are not troubled by things we have forgotten. We accept that memory is imperfect and acknowledge

---

1. De Lepeleire, Heyman and Buntinx, 'The Early Diagnosis of Dementia.'

that remembering everything in detail would likely prove more of a burden than a blessing. We need to edit our own lives. Science accounts for some aspects of recollection and editing, recognising that heightened emotion may well account for the *reminiscence bump* which means we are more able to recollect our late teens and twenties than any other period of our past. There is also scientific consensus that childhood amnesia is an almost universal phenomenon, with most of us remembering nothing before ages four to seven.[2]

Holes in our memories are clearly a normal part of being human. I can't remember when I shifted from aiding and abetting Kathleen in our quest to deny the likelihood of Alzheimer's, to a role predicated on acceptance, accommodation and medical intervention. There must have been a visit to the doctor and a referral for further investigation, but I have no recollection of it. Perhaps at that stage Kathleen was still managing some of her own appointments, maybe I wasn't even there. Perhaps optimism was still competing with reality, and my memory has merged that visit with many others made to the same doctor; after all, no diagnosis was made then. Seeing her GP was simply the mechanism for opening the door to the possibility of a problem.

What I distinctly remember are the subsequent steps to Kathleen's diagnosis, beginning with a home visit by a professional from the memory clinic team. We sat, me, the tester and Kathleen, in Kathleen's tidy, clean and ordered lounge with its green carpet, G-Plan chairs and a coffee table weighted down with her vast stash of *Good Housekeeping, Woman and Home* and *Hello* magazines. We sipped tea and ate the chocolate biscuits I had bought.

I can admit now, that over the years of shopping together, I began to realise that not only was Kathleen no longer capable of remembering what she needed, she also struggled with knowing where she needed to go to get it, and crucially, how to pay. I had, without really noticing the passage of time, moved from taxi, to companion, to personal assistant. Now, faced with a formal visitor, one only I could remember was coming and why, I knew what Kathleen would want. Relationship kicked in. Years of friendship prior to her memory depletion meant that I knew her personality, her character. The chocolate digestives were testimony to the hospitality

2. Østby and Østby, *Adventures in Memory*, 205–8.

she would have given. They were a way of preserving her dignity. Kathleen had a visitor and special effort would be made.

Our tester was a very friendly woman. She explained why she was there, and she asked Kathleen if she was happy to answer a few questions and complete some tasks that might be able to assess how well her memory was working.

'That all seems fine,' Kathleen replied, leaning forward in her chair.

To an onlooker, the situation might have looked faintly ridiculous. Though I had answered the door and made the necessary introductions, Kathleen had responded with politeness and interest and welcomed the woman into her home. She had made small talk over tea and biscuits and responded appropriately to the instructions and explanations. Surely there couldn't be much wrong with the neurology of someone so capable of participating in conversation with a stranger? Surely the test wasn't really needed?

I know now that conversational skill does not necessarily deteriorate rapidly with the onset of Alzheimer's. Kathleen, eight years after diagnosis, was still fully capable of enjoying a chat. It was only when in her company for more than a few minutes that it was evident the talk was circular, that we had been there before. Repeated or looped conversation can be indicative of the pathology associated with dementia. Even after his surgery, Henry Molaison was quite capable of sticking to the topic of conversation, revealing effective short-term memory.[3] Short-term memory is, however, very short. It can be defined as that which we remember in the moment – facts such as an address, phone number or name that is needed immediately and then forgotten. To move any fact, experience or idea to permanent memory, we need to rehearse the information. This he could not do. Short-term memory can only hold about seven items for no more than twenty to thirty seconds at a time, but this is enough to make most conversations fully accessible.[4] Conversational input is rarely above thirty seconds, so Kathleen was able to respond appropriately to verbal stimuli. If asked a question, providing she wasn't distracted, then she could formulate a cohesive reply.

Crucially, once the initial stages of interaction have passed, someone with Alzheimer's will no longer be able to access the

3. Østby and Østby, *Adventures in Memory*.
4. HowStuffWorks , 'Short and Long Term Memory.'

beginning of the conversation and may well repeat themselves. Memories do not remain in the hippocampus, where they are initially received, but need to spread out across the cortex. The complex connections required to store all that makes a memory – smells, tastes, sounds, moods and images – only become established in the brain through a process of maturation.[5] Damage to the hippocampal or limbic region of the brain interferes with the transfer from very short-term memory into something more concrete. This manifests in malfunction in the maturing phase, and thus conversations and events are lost.

Alzheimer's and most other forms of dementia are initially tested for using a simple memory test. To the uninitiated, this needs some explanation. Known as the MMSE – the Mini-Mental State Examination, it is designed to be a quick indicator of cognitive decline. The process takes about fifteen minutes and requires the person being assessed to answer simple questions and perform basic tasks. It begins with the tester, a person from the community memory team or a GP, giving a name, a road and a town. It can be as ordinary as Mr Peters, 12 Seaview Road, Bournemouth. This is repeated a couple of times, and the person being tested is asked to recall it immediately. With its reliance on short-term memory, Kathleen did well at this stage of the test. In the moment, she was fine. The next instruction is to store that information for later. The same is repeated with a list of three commonplace words or objects.

As early as 1988, a research paper identified that there is often a 'distinction between the cognitive self which may be affected by memory loss and the experiencing, feeling self which may be much less impaired.'[6] This was evident as I watched Kathleen take the test. She was secure enough in her understanding of who she was to believe herself capable of following the instructions and performing well. Prior experience had taught her that tests and exams reinforced her abilities rather than revealing their deficit. She would be fine.

After the address has been given, there are many further tasks to perform – the drawing of a clock face and various shapes, general knowledge questions to answer, such as who the Prime Minister is and what day of the week it might be, and some language testing. All these tasks serve to focus attention away from the initial address

5. Østby and Østby, *Adventures in Memory*.
6. Gearing et al., *Mental Health Problems in Old Age*.

and list of three items, causing them to fade immediately from the short-term memory store. On the face of it, this seems cruel, setting up for almost guaranteed failure. But the fact that Alzheimer's impairs the production of new memories means that the process is far less distressing for the one being tested than those who are witnessing the stark reality of neurological atrophy play out in front of them. Kathleen had consented to the test, fully understanding in the moment of consent why it was taking place. Such comprehension was the product of her short-term memory, and as she attempted each task, focused and absorbed, the bigger picture was lost.

Kathleen enjoyed the test. She had always liked a bit of medical attention, and as her career demonstrated, she was not averse to examinations. When she struggled to find an answer, she was distracted by the next question and so promptly forgot any experience of difficulty or failure.

To witness the test is another matter. My friend Jayne told me that it was the worst day of her life:

'To watch my most capable mother – she had been a maths teacher, for goodness' sake – fail to draw a clock face, whilst I had to sit and not look appalled and sit and be encouraging and sit and feel like the woman on whom I had depended, who had loved me and made things alright was disappearing under the influence of a pen and paper and a bloody address … I cannot describe the agony.'[7]

She couldn't bear to see her mother fail. Presented with such stark evidence of decline meant being forced to confront a new reality – the poles had shifted as the parent-child relationship tilted on its axis.

As I sat beside Kathleen, I experienced none of the pain that my friend Jayne described. Crucially, Kathleen was not my mother. Deeply fond of her, there was love between us, but she was not someone on whom I had ever depended. For me, she was not being significantly reduced; her role in my life was not becoming less. As she enjoyed the test, I found myself fascinated by what she could and couldn't remember. She sat forward in her chair, fully attentive to each instruction. I mirrored her, in my matching chair, jotting notes for Philip and trying to fathom what was going on in her brain. The teachers in both of us found the whole scenario compelling.

7. Martin, EF interview.

Friendship, rather than a familial bond, protected us then and continued to protect us through the next decade. Kathleen, who didn't want to be a burden to her nephews with her care, didn't need to feel guilty that she was burdening me – because we were friends, I had chosen to love her; I was not obligated to do so.

I was also protected from the full extent of the grieving process that an Alzheimer diagnosis can precipitate – having met Kathleen when she was already several years into a long retirement, the only comparison I could make to her vibrant youth and capable middle years was through photographs and anecdotal trips down memory lane.

Kathleen was unable to remember the details given to her at the start of the test.

'I don't think you told me an address,' she replied with confidence, certain she was right.

The test was not a reassurance. It rarely is. Despite remembering one of the three items, her clock face was squiggly, and she had no idea of the date or the day. She confirmed who I was and that we were in her living room, but it was clear that these successes were not enough to indicate normal cognitive function.

Kathleen could not remember who the woman was or why she was with us. She couldn't remember why she had done a test, and, after a second round of tea and biscuits, had forgotten the testing process altogether.

For most people who seek help from a GP, the testing process really serves as confirmation of what family and friends already know, and have done, deep-down for some weeks and months, perhaps even years. When the point of testing is reached, most people have already acknowledged, ignored, colluded and then re-acknowledged that there is a problem. A point has been reached. Denial and collusion are no longer feasible.

An MRI scan was the next step to see the activity in the brain and confirm diagnosis of Alzheimer's. The MMSE was not definitive, but the woman from the memory clinic was as sure as she could be that something wasn't quite right. She addressed her comments to Kathleen, but nodded in my direction, recognising that I was writing everything down, a tacit acknowledgement that I was the one who would do the remembering.

When we shut the front door, Kathleen remarked only on the kindness of the visitor, accompanied by a vague concern that she didn't really know who she had been.

Diagnosis can be a frightening moment of confirmation. Alzheimer's disease is readily associated with memory loss, though there are many other signs and symptoms, but it is the memory deficit that equates, for many people, with loss of self. Because Alzheimer's causes cell death in the brain, all symptoms involve some form of cognitive deficit. There are likely to be meaningful reductions in the capacity to establish new learning and significant deficits in the areas of recall, comprehension and use of language. Semantic memory and the higher-order functions of abstract reasoning and attention are also compromised.[8] In the later stages of Alzheimer's, inability to access procedural memory means that basic functions of hygiene, eating and swallowing can also be lost.

The effect of memory loss on identity generates the most fear. When the loss of 'the continuous *I am* thread, first spun from the strands of infancy, becomes disturbed, fades from view or is fragmented, dementia interrupts one's sense of self.'[9]

In the early days of Alzheimer's, Kathleen had some awareness that her lifelong self-perception was failing to match her current capabilities. She knew that she could no longer approach daily tasks such as shopping, cooking and financial management with the confidence she had previously shown. She could no longer assert 'I am independent' or 'I am capable.' In the weeks leading up to diagnosis and for a long while afterwards, her most frequent assertion was 'I am so confused,' and 'I don't understand what's happening to me,' explaining to me that her thinking felt foggy and muddled. Such feelings are typical of the impairment in thought processing, reasoning capacity and fluency of ideas that accompany the more commonly recognised symptoms of memory loss.[10] Kathleen's deep-seated sense of self was being hugely disrupted by the cellular damage in her brain.

Diagnosis can provide those living with the disease with welcome explanation for their confusion, but the lack of effective treatment means fear often overrides this. Historically, doctors

---

8. Segal, Qualls and Smyer, *Aging and Mental Health.*

9. Gearing et al., *Mental Health Problems in Old Age.*

10. Wattis and Curran, *Practical Psychiatry of Old Age.*

have been reluctant to name the disease, preferring euphemisms such as *memory difficulties* to avoid the emotionally loaded label of Alzheimer's disease.[11] Both clinicians and family members worry that knowing the diagnosis may increase anxiety in the person with dementia, but there is also concern about the social stigma that still remains attached to the disease.[12] As adults, we all have rights to access our own medical records, and yet knowledge is not always empowering. I discussed this with a GP in Winchester. He explained that breaking the news is difficult and acknowledged that receiving a diagnosis is not necessarily the best thing for everyone.

'Diagnosis gives access to medicine which can provide reassurance, but the drugs don't work for everyone and they're not a cure.' He went on to say that for some patients 'realising they have Alzheimer's is the beginning of a downward spiral. They give up, assuming their life is over.' [13]

It is, however, generally accepted that full disclosure is best. The current guidelines provided by the National Institution for Health Care and Excellence (NICE) are clear, stating that there is a definite duty to disclose unless there is compelling justification for not doing so.[14] Elaine Robinson, diagnosed with early-onset Alzheimer's aged forty-two, agrees: 'It is a devastating thing to have to face, but we can do it with dignity, and a voice.'[15] James McKillop, also diagnosed in his forties, said, 'Being told of diagnosis at the right time, in the right place, by the right person who has thoughtfully allowed plenty of time for explanations and any questions is essential. Most people can start to confront a problem once they know and understand exactly what it is. If not told the blunt truth, or if the issue is fudged, you are still in the dark, weaponless, fighting the unknown.'[16]

The issue of the right time is pertinent. Alzheimer's disease is often preceded by mild cognitive impairment – deficits that can be readily compensated for so that daily living is not noticeably

---

11. Wilkinson, *The Perspectives of People with Dementia: Research Methods and Motivations*.

12. Waldemar and Burns, *Alzheimer's Disease*.

13. Collins, GP interview.

14. 'Dementia-Short-Guide.Pdf,' Nuffield Bioethics.

15. Wilkinson, *The Perspectives of People with Dementia: Research Methods and Motivations*.

16. Wilkinson, *The Perspectives of People with Dementia: Research Methods and Motivations*.

disrupted. Presence of mild cognitive impairment (MCI) has been shown to form the pre-clinical phase of the disease in many of those who go on to develop Alzheimer's or other forms of dementia.[17] Research surrounding disclosure acknowledges that there may well be times when it is too early for someone to hear their diagnosis recognising that a *timely* diagnosis for most people will be the point when cognitive impairments begin to have a significant, measurable effect on their lives or those of their family.[18]

For Kathleen, diagnosis was handled sensitively and in person. The woman from the memory clinic made a follow-up visit in Kathleen's home, and ensured I would be there too. She gently reminded Kathleen that she had taken part in a memory test and had subsequently attended a hospital appointment with another friend. We both knew that such preamble was necessary – Kathleen had no memory of either part of the diagnostic process. The news was inevitable, but not for Kathleen. Despite the concerns she had expressed and the articles she had saved, her short-term memory was already deteriorating rapidly, and she had no recollection of that prior concern. Fixing Kathleen with kindly eyes, the woman from the memory clinic leaned in and gave the diagnosis,

'I'm afraid you do have Alzheimer's.'

Kathleen's default character kicked in. She showed no sense of dread or horror, but responded with polite courtesy. She asked relevant questions,

'What does this mean for me now?'

The answer was reassuring. There was medication Kathleen could take and as long as she was happy and confident in her own home, there was little need for her to change anything about her life. A letter would be posted to confirm diagnosis from the neurologist who had conducted her MRI scan but, in the meantime, an additional appointment to discuss medication would be set up.

Like before, we shared tea and biscuits with the woman from the memory team, and I showed her out. This time, I felt a bit battered and bruised. Even though the news was nothing other than expected, it was still a blow. Despite reassurances, I knew that Kathleen's life was going to change, and the course of change was not yet mapped. I sat with Kathleen for longer than usual and

17. Waldemar and Burns, *Alzheimer's Disease*.
18. 'Dementia-Short-Guide.Pdf,' Nuffield Bioethics.

made sure she was alright. She was stoic. At some level she knew she lacked her former confidence and competence. She knew that writing everything down wasn't allaying her anxieties, and she knew that she felt frequently muddled and confused. She no longer looked forward to seeing former colleagues because she was fearful of letting herself down, of giving herself away, and she was already beginning to say that she didn't know what she would do without me. So, the diagnosis confirmed that she had been right to cut out articles about dementia from *The Times*. She had Alzheimer's and now we would deal with it. She understood the diagnosis and felt secure she would be looked after. Between us we could work things out.

Such stoicism was short-lived and this was to be the beginning of my journey along a very steep learning curve. I had not yet begun to understand the myriad of detriments associated with the disease. Diagnosis for Kathleen meant that she, in the moment, was better able to understand her confusions. Beyond that, she was left alone with her thoughts and with a reality that was more compromised than any she had previously navigated.

When I popped in a few days later, she was more distressed than I had ever seen. Her hair was uncombed, and her face streaked with tears. This was not a version of Kathleen I had witnessed before. Wild with anxiety, she grasped my arm as she opened the door,

'I'm so glad you're here,' she gasped through tears. 'How did you know I would need you right at this moment?'

She pulled me into the house and clutched onto me as we moved towards the lounge. I tried to sit her down, but she was too agitated.

'I cannot believe it,' she began.

'Believe what?' I encouraged, trying to fathom this sudden change.

She opened her left hand to reveal a crushed and beleaguered letter. It had an NHS logo on the top. Realisation of its contents made me feel sick.

'I received this in the post this morning,' she managed to explain, waving it under my face. 'I have Alzheimer's. How can this be? There is nothing like this in my family. I have Alzheimer's.' At this, she folded herself into her armchair and sobbed into her hands.

'It's alright, Kathleen. We can face this together.'

I sat close and stroked her arm until she composed herself. Taking the letter from her, I hid behind euphemism.

'It just means that you sometimes have memory problems, and I can help you with that. We'll be fine.'

One of the problems with Alzheimer's is that new information is not retained. The fact of her diagnosis was real only in the moment of delivery; it was not a defining factor in her daily life. The MMSE test, the MRI scan and the follow-up visit had all fallen into a black hole where memory used to be. The subsequent letter was something Kathleen was totally unprepared for. How could she begin to adapt to and accommodate a disease that she couldn't even remember she had?

But Kathleen had coping mechanisms. For many weeks, maybe even months and longer, she had been concerned about her own cognition. She had adapted as far as she was able. She wrote notes, used her diary. Her default when her memory seemed fuzzy was to jot things down. Unknown to me was the fact that after she received the letter confirming her diagnosis, she had made a little card for herself that read: *I have Alzheimer's. This means that I will forget things.* She kept it deep in her handbag.

Several weeks after the confirmation letter arrived, it seemed we were settling into a routine. I continued to visit each day, we wrote in the diary when we were going shopping, when there were GP appointments. The medication hadn't yet arrived, and we seemed to be managing just fine. The fact of diagnosis hadn't actually changed anything very much at all.

Then Kathleen unearthed her own note. I was greeted at the door with an almost facsimile response – tears, fears and questions of 'How can I have come to this?' and 'Is this right?'

Kathleen was rediscovering the fact of her diagnosis with the same emotional rawness she had experienced when she received the letter from the consultant, but this time it was her own handwriting that was betraying her sense of self. Shock and anxiety were as palpable this time as they had been weeks before. She had no idea of her own dementia unless forced to confront it. I have no idea if she suffered such agonies on her own when I wasn't around to reassure her. How many times had she unearthed her note to self when I didn't happen to turn up at the door? How many times had she cried alone, unable to think straight enough to pick up the phone? All I could do was scour the bungalow for further notes and correspondence and take them away. They were not useful.

'You're fine,' I smiled at her, holding firmly onto her hand. 'You have me to look after you, and Philip. Terence will be coming down to stay with you soon too.'

Refocusing on her nephew and brother enabled me to shift her thoughts.

Her distress was short-lived. Without evidence of the note, she forgot that she had been upset. She began to speak of her family with affection and look forward to their visit.

Together, Philip and I decided that we needed to be honest with Kathleen, to preserve her dignity as an intelligent woman. Alzheimer's does not destroy past relationship – we knew Kathleen and we wanted any decision over her care to acknowledge and honour who she had been throughout her adult life. Such reaching into character and personality has been shown to aid preservation of a sense of self in the accommodation of Alzheimer's.[19] We decided that whenever she asked why she was confused or had difficulty recalling something, we would tell her gently – explain that she had Alzheimer's, and that was okay, because she also had friends and family who loved her. This worked. No lies were being told and yet no evidence of her condition was left for her to rediscover on her own.

---

19.   Gearing et al., *Mental Health Problems in Old Age.*

5
A Spoonful of Sugar

Formal diagnosis of the disease is inevitably a point of medicalisation, and, although there is no cure for dementia, GPs have a variety of drugs they can offer. At best, medication can arrest the development of the disease and potentially slow down its progress for a limited period of time, but it cannot give back memory function that has already been lost. Most pills have warnings of possible loss of appetite or associated depression.

Kathleen had no qualms about entrusting herself to her doctor – in every conversation she listened intently, understood in the moment what was being offered, and was eager to accept any intervention that might stabilise her condition.

The first course of action was overseen by the local memory clinic. Kathleen was offered a place in group cognitive stimulation sessions. Realising that I was not a family member and that I worked part-time, they were happy to organise transport for Kathleen to attend the group twice a week for a period of seven weeks.

Memory is indeed unreliable. I hadn't remembered this stage in Kathleen's Alzheimer journey until my research stumbled on the NICE guidelines for those newly diagnosed. Reading about the therapy offered on the NHS prompted one of those moments when something buried deep in the synapses is woken up and reinvigorated. Having not thought about the sessions for years, I recalled Kathleen getting rather excited about them. She took them very seriously, and the sheets she brought home with her testified to application of the concentration and diligence that had typified her former studies and career.

My only role in these sessions was to ensure that they were marked in her diary and on her wall calendar in the kitchen. The drivers knew their clients all had early diagnoses of Alzheimer's and had mild to moderate dementia. If they turned up to the house and Kathleen was not ready, I'd been reassured that they would explain why they were there and would wait for her to gather her things. This was my first experience of entrusting her to strangers and they made it very easy for me.

Group therapy is designed to be fun and sociable, providing a safe space for those who have recently found out that they are living with dementia to speak out about their concerns. Each session covers a different theme, so there is never any pressure to recall material from previous weeks. Continuity and context are provided by the homogeneous structure of the sessions. At the beginning of every meeting there is a warm-up activity, a song and a 'reality orientation board.' This board contains key information such as date, time, place, weather and names of each participant. The activities that follow are designed to stimulate thinking, memory and socialisation.

Kathleen never remembered attending the sessions or what she had done in them, but her attitude to seeing the dates in her diary was always positive. I assume therefore that she enjoyed discussing current news stories, listening to music or singing, playing word games and baking. I only know that these are the activities on offer because I looked up Cognitive Stimulation Therapy sessions on the internet.[1] Looking back, Kathleen's inability to report back should have been clear indication that her dementia was already tipping from mild to moderate, but this wasn't something I was looking for. Despite the diagnosis, I was still colluding in the idea that life could carry on as normal.

If I ever found notes or worksheets from the stimulation sessions, I asked her about them.

'It was all very informative, as you can see,' she replied, indicating the paper.

---

1. Comas-Herrera and Knapp, 'Cognitive Stimulation Therapy (CST): Summary of Evidence on Cost-Effectiveness,' 1.

It's interesting that when we are not involved in something, we can more readily dismiss it. The cognitive therapy had been organised by the memory clinic. I had nothing to do with it at all. Because I didn't know what Kathleen was doing there or any of the people involved, I had no way of successfully opening a conversation with her about what she had done. I had no cues to give. Without cues, Kathleen could no longer converse in any detail or at any length. She could certainly no longer initiate discussion on experiences that she had encountered independently. Amazingly, this didn't worry me at all. I compartmentalised the activity as something outside our mutual experience and therefore not fully relevant in my ongoing assessment of how she was managing. This is probably the reason why I had forgotten the provision of the sessions until now.

Aside from cognitive group therapy, diagnosis also prompted the opportunity for chemical intervention. Crucially, all drugs provided for dementia are compounds designed to act on the brain. One of the current theories of the aetiology of Alzheimer's disease is the amyloid hypothesis, based on the idea that there is greater build-up of the protein, beta amyloid peptide (sometimes known as plaque) in the brain of someone with Alzheimer's disease.[2] What this means for the layperson is that scientists believe that Alzheimer's is likely to be caused either by over-production of beta amyloid or a reduction in the brain's capacity to clear the protein effectively.[3]

A former theory that still holds interest for research is the cholinergic hypothesis, whereby damage to acetyl cholinergic neurons is seen in patients with Alzheimer's.[4] Scientists have identified damage to these neurons as a potential early indicator of the disease.[5] Acetylcholine improves the brain's ability to process information and increases alertness and attention. It is processed in the area of the brain associated with emotion and memory processing – the amygdala, hippocampus and temporal lobe – precisely the areas Scoville operated on in his treatment of Henry Molaison. It has been seen that when this area of the brain fails to function, confusion, disorientation and emotional disruption are likely.[6]

---

2. Wattis and Curran, *Practical Psychiatry of Old Age*.

3. Waldemar and Burns, *Alzheimer's Disease*.

4. Taylor, *The Fragile Brain*.

5. Schliebs and Arendt, 'The Cholinergic System in Aging and Neuronal Degeneration.'

6. Taylor, *The Fragile Brain*.

Understanding brain function and failure in these terms has led to four key antidementia drugs being used for mild to moderate forms of Alzheimer's disease. The first three, *donepezil, rivastigmine and galantamine,* are all cholinesterase inhibitors that prevent the breakdown of acetylcholine.[7] The fourth drug, *memantine,* acts on glutamate pathways – those neurotransmitters released by the nervous system and responsible for sending signals between nerve cells[8] – and is most often used as an alternative for patients who are intolerant of the cholinesterase inhibitors.[9]

All drugs carry some risks, and NICE guidelines state that antidementia drugs can only be prescribed after meeting the following criteria:

- A patient must be diagnosed with mild to moderate Alzheimer's disease
- The drug(s) may only be prescribed by a specialist: old age psychiatrist, geriatrician or neurologist
- A patient must be carefully monitored after commencing treatment
- A review of drug efficacy must take place at between 2-4 months with a view to withdrawing treatment around the third month if no improvement in cognitive function is evidenced.[10]

Following her memory test and subsequent MRI scan, Kathleen met the criteria for medical treatment for her Alzheimer's. In discussion with her family, she decided to take the drugs.

Prescribed with *donepezil,* I agreed to be the responsible carer who would ensure that she took the drugs as directed. Previously, Kathleen had experienced unusual dizziness and fatigue, and she complained that it felt as though her heart was working too hard. Looking at the possible side effects of her blood pressure meds, it seemed plausible that she had been taking them too frequently, forgetting she had had her dose with breakfast and was taking another at lunchtime. A simple plastic dispenser, marked clearly with the days of the week, had provided an easy solution to the

7. Wattis and Curran, *Practical Psychiatry of Old Age.*

8. 'About Glutamate Toxicity,' Stanford University.

9. Wattis and Curran, *Practical Psychiatry of Old Ag.e*

10. '1 Guidance | Donepezil, Galantamine, Rivastigmine and Memantine for the Treatment of Alzheimer's Disease | Guidance.' NICE: Wattis and Curran, *Practical Psychiatry of Old Age.*

problem. Kathleen could see that she had taken her Monday morning doses because the tablets were gone. I filled the dispenser up every Friday and kept the rest of the pills at my house to avoid a repeat of unwitting overdosage. When they were gone, they had been taken. Such brilliant contraptions and devices are only effective, however, when you can remember what day of the week it is. Kathleen quickly learnt to cross-check that detail with firstly her diary and then the newspaper. Providing it was the right newspaper for the right day on top of the pile, then that worked. Many families I spoke to acknowledged that the pill dispensing system is severely limited for those living alone with Alzheimer's. This simple daily task can become fraught with difficulty.

We were not yet at this stage. Her compensatory mechanisms were still working, and Kathleen was able, by and large, to check the day off with some accuracy. A woman of routine and timetables, she had a wealth of lifetime experience to draw upon. Until now, however, any miscalculation involved drugs with only limited side effects. I was much more nervous about pills that acted on brain function.

Donepezil can only be prescribed by a specialist. For us this meant that Kathleen's supplies were posted directly to her from the hospital pharmacy. Logistically, this was difficult. Aside from the tablets in the dispenser, I was already keeping spare drugs at my house to keep Kathleen safe. I now had to be extra vigilant; pills were supplied on a monthly basis and I needed to make sure I was aware when they were likely to be sent so that I could intercept them and thus keep her safe. They could not be sent to my house as I had no power of medical attorney. Philip and Matthew, who did have such legal powers, were too far away to be of practical use regarding the distribution of the drug. *Donepezil* has a long list of potential side effects and it is essential that patients start on a lower dose to build their tolerance. Reluctant to trust this drug to the daily dispenser system, I visited each morning to supervise the taking of the pills.

Despite all these precautions, this was not a happy time. After the initial doses had been taken, I saw changes in Kathleen which alarmed me. She became increasingly muddled and lethargic, and needed continual reassurance. It was not going to be enough to visit her each day and so I began popping in at lunchtime and again in the evening. The drugs were affecting Kathleen's personality in a way that, so far, Alzheimer's had not. She didn't get dressed, she didn't brush her hair, and she didn't eat. She was sad, weepy and continually complained of feeling tired and ill.

I was losing my friend.

Even more distressing than the manifestations of the side effects, was the confusion that accompanied it. She would ask me repeatedly, 'Why am I feeling like this?' and then her words became more emotive and melodramatic, 'I feel absolutely dreadful,' and 'I can't go on like this.'

It was so difficult to watch these changes in her character that I wanted to stop the pills immediately. I contacted Philip, and we talked about what might be the best course of action for Kathleen. The doctors and memory clinic staff had warned us that the first few weeks on the tablets could be tough. If I could just get Kathleen through twenty-one days, then things should settle. Philip was mindful that his aunt had never been averse to medical intervention; he thought that, in the days when Kathleen had had the capacity to see potential longer-term benefits, then she would be insisting on seeing the first three weeks through to their completion. I knew he was right, but the problem was that she no longer had such capacity. It had gone. All she had was the present and all she knew was that she felt dreadful.

Philip was inclined to cling to his prior knowledge of Kathleen's character and keep going for a while. I agreed to support any decision he made. So when Kathleen was distressed, I repeatedly explained that the pills were being taken to help her memory, and that her body needed time to get used to them. In the moment, she accepted that, but, within minutes, all she knew was the confusion, nausea and bleak depression that the pills shrouded her in. It was impossible for her to grasp any sense of the long view. Long-term had been rendered conceptually meaningless in her cognitively compromised brain.

Perhaps surprisingly, this was the first time we wept together. I mourned her decline from that upright lady across the church hall to a shuffling, green velour dressing-gown woman whose hair was uncombed and whose eyes were frightened. She wept with fear and confusion. She could not comprehend what was happening. All she knew was that she had 'never felt this way before.'

I called Philip again and he made an emergency visit to the south of England. Like me, he was appalled.

'I hadn't imagined it was this bad,' he admitted.

It is often the small things that floor us into recognition that all is not as it should be.

'She always gets dressed, no matter what,' he said.

This simple statement contained layers of pain as he saw his aunt for the first time with new eyes. Kathleen was vulnerable and she was suffering.

He spent the day with her, holding her hand, reassuring her. With his support, she got dressed and picked at the food he provided. She looked brighter when I visited that afternoon, and we dared to hope that she might be through the worst.

She wasn't. It was Philip's constant company which had made her pain and confusion bearable. He had been able to provide a continual drip of encouragement to get her through the day. Once he returned home, there was no way I could manage to be with Kathleen twenty-four seven for the remaining days of the initial three-week period.

We ended the trial by tablets when she leant on her sink in the kitchen and cried, 'No more of those. I can't take any more of those.' She had begun to make a link between the pills and her feelings of despair. Enough of her brain circuitry was firing to enable an instinctive understanding that the *donepezil* was responsible for her wretchedness. I tried once more to reassure her and explain that we were halfway through the process, that, ultimately, they might be beneficial. Presenting her with halfway was, however, like presenting her with Everest without oxygen. She simply couldn't bear to try.

At this point I longed to go back to the relative simplicity of short-term memory loss. Suddenly Alzheimer's seemed far less menacing than its medication.

With another phone call, I got Philip's blessing to stop the tablets. Together, Kathleen and I washed the remaining pills down the sink and sat, exhausted, in the living room. For Kathleen, there was brief relief, soon forgotten as the drugs worked their way out of her system. For me, and for Kathleen's family, there was the burden of realisation that perhaps medical intervention would not be appropriate for her, that there was little alternative but to leave her at the mercy of a disease that was quietly advancing on her neuronal system.

Kathleen was obviously sensitive to the impact of the brain-altering chemicals and it wasn't worth the price. Over a year later, she was newly resident in a care home and Philip, in consultation with the matron-in-charge, decided that it was worth trying again with a second drug, *galantamine*. In this context Kathleen would have access to round-the-clock reassurance and support from medical staff that I hadn't been able to provide the first time. The results were the same, surprising matron by Kathleen's swift change of character. After that, she remained drug-free until her death.

It is important at this point in our story to reassure readers that our experience of the available dementia medicines is not everyone's. Friends shared very different tales.

'There were absolutely no side effects at all,' Jayne explained, slightly perplexed that I had even asked the question.

Her mother's cognition seemed to improve immediately, and she noted that conversations on the phone were brighter, more cohesive.[11] Another friend attributed the success of *donepezil* for her mother's continued stability and independence for 'a good two to three years after diagnosis.'[12]

For Kathleen, it was different. Seeing her on medication had brought his aunt's vulnerability home to Philip. Although she seemed safe in her bungalow just a few streets away from me, he wanted to prepare for the future. The facts were stark. Kathleen had a brother just four years her junior who lived with his wife in Derbyshire; her two nephews lived and worked in Exeter and Nottingham respectively – and that was the sum total of her family. Kathleen had spent her entire adult life in Maidenhead and could not conceive of moving away from everything and everyone she had known over many decades. She was staying in the south-east. Should she ever need more care, and this seemed likely, then a local residential home was the only feasible option. With his brother, Philip began to investigate the possibility of care homes.

---

11. Martin, EF interview.
12. Martin, MH interview.

6
Personal Histories, Changing Times

Kathleen's life was a homage to the safety and reliability of routine. She liked to plan and have control over her time and activities. That pattern was set in childhood; as a young girl, she worked hard at school, happy to learn and do her homework. Family life was disciplined, working around her father's shifts in the police force. Church punctuated the weekend as did regular Sunday dinners with her grandparents. Once she had secured permission to have piano lessons, Kathleen loved them. From the beginning, she decided to make music into a pastime, never wanting to take exams. It was only when she opted for Music for her Higher School Certificate that she realised she needed Grade 6 Piano to qualify. Pragmatic, she did what was required and passed that exam in order to study what she wanted in the sixth form.

Such methodical diligence was a hallmark of Kathleen's character, and one that would be most challenged by the diagnosis of Alzheimer's disease. Contrary to expectation, it has been suggested that one of the key functions of memory is not to enable us to look back, but to facilitate our ability to look forward and plan for the future. Similar to episodic memory which we use to recall an event or experience, this has been termed episodic foresight.[1] As a species, we use our knowledge of prior experience to enable us

---

1. Suddendorf and Corballis, 'The Evolution of Foresight,' 327.

to plan forward, to imagine the future. In brain scans, the areas active when remembering are almost identical to those involved in imagining.[2] In order to make effective preparation for a future event, we need to be able to imagine likely scenarios and outcomes.

Though primarily associated with the loss of the past, memory deficit may well be the reason that those living with Alzheimer's are less able to plan ahead. Kathleen was living in a world that made less and less sense to her. For someone so entrenched in routine and organisation, it may well be that her inability to think ahead clearly, as much as her incapacity to look back, was responsible for the confusion that she sometimes described as overwhelming.

From her recollections and anecdotes about life as a teacher, it seems that Kathleen's career was wrapped in a schedule that brokered little room for deviation. She moved from being a pupil to a student, and from that to being teacher and deputy head, all of which involved timetables and institutional adherence to routine. She explained to me on many occasions that she would be in school by 8 a.m. and stay until 5 p.m.

'Occasionally I would leave school an hour earlier to have my hair cut,' she said in a tone of confession, before going on to admit, 'I chose the salon across the road from school so that I would waste as little time as possible.'

Evenings were also enshrined in Kathleen-imposed structure.

'I would get home and cook my meal, then I would mark or prepare lessons until the 9 o'clock news. After that, I would go to bed.'

Domestic duties such as shopping, cleaning and ironing all took place at the weekend. Further marking and preparation was allowed on Saturdays, but she insisted on a day of rest, and Sunday was for church, walks and friends.

The chaos of Alzheimer's to someone so immersed in self-discipline can only be imagined. Kathleen was able to explain in her lucid moments, that it was the confusion and muddled thinking that she found the most difficult to accept – she felt as though her brain no longer did her bidding.

Some of the early changes wrought by dementia were subtle. In the kitchen there was a black transistor radio with the dial permanently set to Radio 4. In the time before Alzheimer's, I would

---

2. Schacter, Addis and Buckner, 'Remembering the Past to Imagine the Future,' 658.

be greeted by presenters shouting throughout the bungalow, the volume compensating for Kathleen's poor hearing. It was one of the first things that dementia took away. She would forget that it was there to use and had to be reminded that she enjoyed listening to Today whilst she had her breakfast; and then, quite swiftly, she forgot how to turn it on. The silence was uncanny.

There is a wide gap between normal cognition and dementia that is hard to negotiate. When others advised me that Kathleen would enjoy the radio as a companion for when I couldn't be there, well-wishers were showing investment in the pre-dementia version of Kathleen's character. They were putting her personality before her disease in a way that should be applauded – after all, such accommodation is vital to preservation of selfhood. But with Alzheimer's, helpful ways are rarely the same ways as before. The disease demands continual adaptation. Kathleen's friends could not conceive of a Kathleen who could no longer remember how to turn the radio on and off; they could not adjust their cognition to comprehend hers.

Alzheimer's is isolating. At first, Kathleen drew away from her friends. Initially just quiet in their company, she then avoided social situations where she might not be able to cope as well as she had once done. Whilst not ashamed of her diagnosis, she was certainly embarrassed by the deficits it revealed. Her sense of self was built on competence and independence and she didn't want former friends and colleagues to see her reduced by dementia. And the friends that persisted didn't do so for long. Kathleen had only a couple of regular visitors once she moved to Bluebell House. Fear of dementia is reflected in this withdrawal; for her peers, perhaps it was too much to witness, too hard to adapt to.

Kathleen's radio began to gather dust in the corner of her kitchen. We persisted with television a while longer, but her insistent unplugging of every electrical item before she went to bed meant that she couldn't work out how to put it on again in the morning. Phone calls to say the television was broken, could my husband come and fix it, became a regular occurrence. We often found Kathleen in her chair, pointing a remote control at an unplugged set. At first, to protect her dignity, we pretended some malfunction and reassured her that it was now sorted. As the disease progressed, such dissembling was no longer necessary – by the time he arrived, she was simply delighted to see him. She had completely forgotten the problem with the television that had prompted the call in the first place.

Kathleen's retirement in her late fifties offered the first real opportunity for her to break free from duty and routine. She was deeply proud that her successor as deputy head was to be one of her former pupils taught in her earliest years. Kathleen left behind a legacy that was acknowledged with countless goodbye dinners and gifts. Photographs attest to these events. I see a tall, ginger-haired, bespectacled lady in a full skirt and billowing blouse accepting a portable television, whilst students queued to present bouquets of cellophane-wrapped flowers. I don't recognise this version of her. The images depict another age, a time when I did not know Kathleen, but as she looked at the photos and spoke of 'her girls' and the presents they bestowed upon her, her voice resonated with equal measures of pride and humility.

My experience of Kathleen has been of a practical and unsentimental woman. When recalling her retirement, she always punctuated her story with a sense of wonder:

'And I just walked away. Over thirty years of my life totally taken over by the demands of teaching and running the school, and then nothing. I finished school on a Friday afternoon and I was on an aeroplane within the week. And do you know,' she said, always ending this anecdote with the same tone of incredulity, 'I never once missed it. Not at all. A whole lifetime and I turned my back, walked away and it was done.'

Perhaps one reason why she made this life change with such ease was the fact that she had planned a significant period of foreign travel. In the days before internet booking, she remembered spending weekends channelling her powers of organisation by letter, phone calls and visits to the local Thomas Cook in order to fulfil a lifetime's ambition to see the places that, up until then, she had only taught about. Her photograph albums from this time reflect freedom. There is joy in her face.

Although able to recall her excitement at heading beyond Europe for the first time, remembering details of people and places was sketchy. Kathleen knew she had stayed with friends in Australia but couldn't be certain who. She wasn't entirely sure which continents she had visited, or where one holiday ended, and another memory began. In some conversations she was certain she had been to

Scandinavia, in others, she was unsure whether she had visited Sweden, though she did have a friend who lived there.

This can be explained by the fact that middle-aged memories are often lost as Alzheimer's progresses. Rehearsed less than the remote past, these middle years seem to become vulnerable soon after initial episodic changes are noticed. Perhaps counter-intuitively, our autobiographical memory retains more certainty, the more distant the recollection.[3]

We can be sure that she went to Australia and New Zealand, however, as her stories of adventure retold to a younger Philip, encouraged him and his wife to visit the Antipodes themselves. In a card that Kathleen kept propped on her piano, Philip wrote that his aunt had always been an inspiration and someone that his children looked up to. The desk calendar for 2018 was a photobook gift that depicted Philip recreating tourist snaps that he remembered his aunt sharing with him decades before.

Routine is a close companion. On return from her adventure, Kathleen immediately began to fashion a new shape for her life. Essentially, she recreated a school timetable for her retirement, substituting A-Level classes for duties at St George's Chapel in Windsor, swapping lower school assemblies for piano playing at the old folk's weekday church service and replacing staff rotas with church record-keeping. She spoke to me of this time with conviction. 'It was important not to lose sight of being useful. I didn't want to just sit at home and do the washing.' Here she paused and smiled admitting, 'though I did rather enjoy housework.'

This insight has been recently corroborated by academic research. It seems that in order to age well, to enjoy the longevity associated with modernity, the need to remain useful to other people is paramount. We need a purpose that goes beyond our own confines and can enhance the lives of others.[4] This is hugely disrupted when cognitive impairment combines to make a 'double jeopardy' of old age.[5] Developed societies already marginalise their older citizens, and when those citizens suffer with dementia in any of its forms, then any value they have retained is quickly lost. This is undoubtedly

3. Woods, *Psychological Problems of Ageing – Assessment, Treatment and Care.*

4. BBC Radio 4. 'The Long and Short of Life Expectancy.'

5. Rodeheaver and Datan, 'The Challenge of Double Jeopardy.'

connected to the value we place, as a society, on memory, seeing it not merely as a record of a past, but as intrinsic to our humanity.

Kathleen acquired an invisibility cloak when she was diagnosed with dementia. If we met friends during our tearoom excursions or trips to town, they would smile at her and then immediately turn their full attention on me. Uncertain of how much conversation Kathleen could cope with, most people chose none at all. I now know that when we were out, Kathleen was using all her capacity to cope with surroundings that were increasingly defamiliarised. This meant that she was unable to initiate conversation to put others at ease. When we did stop to chat to someone, Kathleen used years of politeness to wait until they had passed by before asking,

'I think I know that person. Remind me who it was.'

Lack of context makes meaningful interaction very difficult. Families often mourn the fact that their loved one no longer remembers who they are. I have no idea if Kathleen ever forgot my name because I never gave her the chance. As her Alzheimer's advanced, I greeted her very specifically.

'Hi, it's Karen. How are you today?'

Inclusion of my name gave Kathleen immediate context. If she stopped using it voluntarily then I must have chosen not to notice. She certainly never forgot what we meant to each other. Feelings, voices, tones have a deeper history than the mere semantics of names and roles.

When I met Kathleen, she was slowing down, but still had a strong sense of purpose and identity. She had rescinded her role as education officer for St George's Chapel and stood down from her position as trustee of a local housing charity. Routine remained a fixture in her eighth decade – Kathleen would go into town on the bus a couple of days a week and play the piano regularly for the midweek service. She walked each morning for her paper and did the crossword in the afternoons. Certain days remained allocated for shopping and cleaning and laundry. She still drove to church on a Sunday morning, giving up her car just before her eightieth birthday because she didn't think her reactions were as reliable as they once had been.

'I couldn't live with myself if I caused an accident,' she said.

This same pragmatism had seen her remodel her bathroom immediately after retirement, so that she had easy access to the bath. As long as she lived in her bungalow, Kathleen could out-stride me in a walk about town – the mobility aids she had bought to future-proof her house were never necessary, but she bought them just in case. She lived her life independently and took as many precautions as she could against becoming 'a burden' on her family.

This was the version of Kathleen that I knew and loved first.

Accompanying this rich life was a compulsion to record things. Her tiny scrawl covered cash books, address books, calendars, packing lists, birthday lists and shopping lists. Most sacred of all, Kathleen was particularly insistent about her diary, ensuring that it was purchased in October so that early appointments for the following year could be put in.

Alzheimer's wreaked changes here too. Even before she was diagnosed, Kathleen was beginning to lack certainty in what she had written within the pages of the slim week-to-view volume. Looking back, this was clear evidence of mild cognitive impairment that often precedes Alzheimer's. Despite confusion and uncertainty, Kathleen associated the diary with being organised – she couldn't conceive of running an effective life without recourse to its pages. I decided to try and harness this conviction as a prop to outwit memory loss. First, we began to have diary consultations, checking each Friday that her information for the coming week tallied with mine. She needed to know when I would next be coming and what we might be doing.

About the same time as she began to need calendar consultations, I noticed Kathleen's increased bewilderment in her own kitchen. She began to struggle to make tea because she couldn't remember where the tea bags lived or where she kept the cups. It wasn't unusual for her to try several doors before finding what she wanted. Sometimes, in the act of looking, she forgot what she was trying to achieve in the first place.

We added another layer of prompts to her daily routine. Together we made a set of cards that said: Bowls, Plates and Cups; Cereal; Soup and stuck them on the various drawers and cupboards in the kitchen. These helped Kathleen to navigate her own home with some of her former confidence and enabled her to be independent for as long as possible.

Kathleen wrote notes to herself right up until the very advanced stages of Alzheimer's, but even one as innocent as *Do the washing* could fall foul of cognitive failure. Clothes went from the washing machine to the tumble dryer and then to the basket. Instead of being put away, Kathleen would re-read her note and the laundry would be done over and over again. *Buy the paper* was also a case in point. Neighbours plucked up the courage to tell Philip that Kathleen had popped over more than once to give them a free copy of *The Times*. We realised that she must have seen the note, gone for her walk, bought a paper, only to return home and find an identical copy on the coffee table. Finding waste reprehensible, she donated newspapers to the family opposite. At least that note kept her fit.

As her brain function became more muddled, the notes became increasingly obsessive and I learnt to recognise which ones would eventually distress as much as they reassured. Notes which stated *Philip is coming* or *Terence will visit* were the first ones to be culled. Reading them from a previous time, Kathleen would become excited. The house was cleaned and the beds aired, and then she would be disappointed or upset as they failed to arrive.

I wonder about the next generation of retirees. Will they have an increased arsenal with which to fight the vagaries of memory loss? Diagnosed with early-onset dementia, author Wendy Mitchell writes about the usefulness of the internet, an iPad and a camera to help her negotiate life.[6] Brought up with modern technology, will future Alzheimer patients be better equipped to retain their independence for longer?

At every stage, we discussed strategies for remembering. As a team, we plotted new ways for Kathleen to negotiate her old life, to outwit the slowly relentless advance of plaque and tangles in her brain. Fully aware that Kathleen would not recall these conversations, I remain convinced that continued discussion and involvement in her own life and decision-making was a vital component in retaining her autonomy and self-respect. I needed to empower her, or at least not knowingly disempower her. Kathleen was wise, intelligent and immensely capable – Alzheimer's could not rob her of that sense of self.

---

6. Mitchell, *Somebody I Used to Know*, 77.

7
Alarm Bells

Kathleen's sense of self was something we always sought to preserve – Kathleen by instinct, and me perhaps more consciously. Failing to find her through the fog of medication had been my main motivator to give up the *donepezil*. Once the drugs were gone from her system, it was as if she had been rebooted, as if the real Kathleen was given the time and space to be herself, in spite of living with Alzheimer's.

Part of that sense of self was deeply entwined in her capacity to manage her financial affairs, and the weekly visit to the bank was something that she clung onto for a long time. Solely responsible for her own solvency since she left home at eighteen, she took pride and enjoyment in balancing the books. It was inevitable, therefore, that money was something she became very anxious about when she felt her former competence ebbing away. For those living with mild cognitive impairment or the early stages of Alzheimer's, it is common to experience periods of intense frustration and confusion, a time when the person with dementia is acutely aware of the shortcomings in their thinking process.

When she was able to rationalise and describe her feelings, Kathleen voiced fears about a sense of creeping incompetence that was beyond her control. This commonly manifested itself in heightened anxiety, especially when we were outside the safety of home. Aware that she was forgetting things, she focused her worries on the contents of her handbag.

'My cheque book. My dear, I haven't got my cheque book.'

Rummaging through her bag, she channelled her fears towards something tangible, something that she knew was essential for a trip into town. Once she felt the leather cover, soft with years of use, then she relaxed. Fear is, however, more tenacious than that and once reassured about the cheque book, Kathleen worried about her shopping list. Whilst I learnt to have the list in my pocket so that I could produce it with a flourish every time she panicked, I could not assume the same responsibility for her cheques, purse and handbag. There is a thin line between dignity and condescension, and I was very aware of this throughout our friendship. There is an even thinner line between friendship and perceived fraud. I knew that any help I gave Kathleen with financial transactions needed to be completely transparent.

After locking the front door of Kathleen's bungalow, we paused on the porch step so that she could open the navy handbag and check everything was as it should be. It made no difference that we had checked before we left the house – Kathleen had no memory of that. We rifled through the tissues and the ballpoint pens until the familiar battered red cover surfaced. Her cheque book was there. It was safe.

The world is not built for those with dementia, and at the car park we had to negotiate another issue. A disabled person can have a blue badge; parents with small children can access the most convenient spaces. When we took our regular trips to town there were no comparable concessions for those with Alzheimer's, which is why I am thankful that the disabled badge system is now being rolled out to include those with a dementia diagnosis.[1] At first, Kathleen would come with me to the pay station, but the central car park in our town is notoriously unreliable. Sometimes we had to walk to four different locations before one would accept my coins. Negotiating the cars and trying to hold onto Kathleen's arm whilst feeding reluctant machines became more and more difficult. She didn't understand why we needed to take such a tour, becoming agitated in the increasingly unfamiliar surroundings of bleak, grey concrete. It was quicker if I did it on my own, but in order to keep her safe that necessitated locking Kathleen in the car.

---

1. Alzheimer's Society, 'Blue Badge Scheme Extended to People with Hidden Disabilities including People with Dementia.'

'I'm off to get the ticket. Just stay there. You can watch me try all the machines.'

I always explained what I was doing but knew that a few minutes could seem interminable to Kathleen, and I worried that she would become anxious. It reminded me of having toddlers and the faint guilt that followed me whenever I dared leave them in their car seats as I paid for petrol. And I suppose that is essentially what it is like to love and care for someone with Alzheimer's. Although Kathleen was four decades my senior, and most definitely not a child, when we were out, she was as dependent on my care as my children had been when they were small.

Whenever she became anxious or upset, symptoms of Alzheimer's would be more pronounced. Even in a person without dementia, anxiety produces cognitive deficits, with working memory particularly affected.[2] When a person has Alzheimer's, the defamiliarisation of once familiar places and the fear of meeting somebody one no longer recognises renders a normal visit to the High Street fraught. Kathleen repeated herself more in town than she did in the house, seemingly having no capacity to rationalise her fears or hold onto reassurance.

'My cheque book,' she would repeat. 'Have I got my cheque book?'

'It's alright; it's in your handbag. We checked earlier.'

She would nod at me then and clutch my arm a little tighter. Alzheimer's was teaching Kathleen to surrender her independence and replace a lifetime of self-reliance with a deep trust in me. This was likely to have been the first time Kathleen had chosen to fully trust someone who was not family. It was not a choice that she would have made without her dementia diagnosis, but it was a gift from Alzheimer's to us both. The disease enabled a relationship beyond expectation; it stretched the boundaries of friendship and created a bond of love. In the years we negotiated dementia together, I was acutely aware that it was affording our friendship a privilege I valued deeply. Whilst Kathleen could not articulate this, it was evident in her demeanour that she also valued what we meant to each other. Contrary to societal fears that Alzheimer's destroys relationships, it is also possible to read a very different story.

When I knew her first and was simply a friend who drove her into town once a week, I would wait on the blue seats in the bank

2. Moran, 'Anxiety and Working Memory Capacity.'

while Kathleen withdrew her weekly allowance. But it didn't take long before she needed more support. At first, I joined her in the queue and stood next to her as she wrote her cheque, reassuring her that she was doing it right. And then, one day, her pen remained poised as Kathleen seemed to stare blankly at the piece of paper in front of her. She lifted her eyes, scanning the room until they locked onto the familiar logo on the wall.

'I'm in the bank,' Kathleen acknowledged, before turning to me. 'Do I need money? Have I got enough?'

After that, it was our habit to sit together on the blue sofa as Kathleen opened her purse and decided she needed more cash. I would remind her of the shops we needed to visit and advise how much might be required. I queued with her and then she stood quietly before the clerk, smiling and passing the time of day, before looking to me for instruction. I then dictated every word she needed to write – a cheque for cash so that she could be solvent for the week.

That society is not set up to cope with memory loss is perfectly illustrated by modern banking. Kathleen had never joined the chip and pin generation, preferring to write cheques and keep a handwritten record of all expenditure. But, in an increasingly digital age, the tellers needed more than a signature match, and it was clear that they were becoming rightly concerned about Kathleen's capacity to handle her own finances.

In assessment for Alzheimer's, medical practice has been focused on cognitive processing. The MMSE test assesses memory, attention and language. More recently, however, increased attention has been paid to the social deficits that are a consequence of brain atrophy. Known as *Activities of Daily Living* (ADL) or the more advanced *Instrumental Activities of Daily Living* (IADL), professionals can now assess the capacity of a person with Alzheimer's to retain independence.[3] ADLs include basic functions such as washing, dressing and feeding oneself, and these, though increasingly challenging in moderate Alzheimer's disease, are not usually severely impacted until later, more advanced stages of dementia. IADL's encompass more sophisticated tasks like handling money, shopping, cooking, taking medication and driving.[4]

---

3. Segal, Qualls and Smyer, *Aging and Mental Health*.
4. Segal, Qualls and Smyer.

Kathleen had given up her driving licence some years before diagnosis and we had already put a system in place for ensuring that she took her blood pressure tablets safely. As far as shopping was concerned, I had gradually become more involved as she became less confident, but it was still Kathleen who stood with her purse at the checkout and handed over her own money. She was still competent at transactional conversations and her working memory was enough to cope with the brevity of exchanges likely to occur at a till point. But financial competence is far more than handling cash transactions. Financial capacity comprises a wide range of abilities that are both conceptual and practical. They require sound judgement and are critical to the maintenance of independence in society.[5] Kathleen's capacity to handle her own affairs was about to be called into question.

One Friday as we stood at the counter, a member of staff apologised to us, saying that it was clear that Kathleen didn't really know what she was doing, that I might be open to accusations of coercion if they didn't step in. It was alright as long as there were staff members who remembered her, recognised her as a genuine customer, but the staff were changing. Turnover was high. Soon the whole branch would be self-service and PIN dependent. Wasn't there a family member who could arrange cash for her?

Kathleen was feisty. Even in the closing stages of the disease, she occasionally resurfaced from confusion with a wry observation or indignant comment. In the bank, on that Friday, she excelled,

'I have been coming here since 1952. I don't expect to have difficulty in getting my money out.'

The teller was kind but firm.

'I realise you have been coming here a long time. I recognise you and your friend here, and you can have your money today. But you need to think about the future.' She trailed off, looking uncomfortable.

I reassured Kathleen. We would chat to Philip, sort something out. Part of Kathleen's pragmatism had meant that on her retirement she had written a will and organised Philip and Matthew to be her powers of attorney in matters of finance should the need ever arise. Perhaps now was the time to start thinking about such things. But Kathleen wasn't emotionally ready to surrender control over her

---

5. Larrabee, *Forensic Neuropsychology*.

money. Never having been married she had never shared financial responsibilities and burdens. Every house move, car purchase and investment decision had been hers and hers alone. She identified as an intelligent, capable woman and she still perceived herself as competent to handle her own affairs.

For those living with Alzheimer's, the gap between perception of competence and its practical outworking can be distorted. As it is common to lose a sense of time, those with dementia often perceive themselves as a younger version than that which the years dictate. This naturally assumes unquestionable competence in activities of daily living.

Despite reluctance to accept someone questioning her financial competency, it was clear something had to be worked out. Kathleen needed money on a weekly basis, and soon the avenue we had been relying on would be closed. It was decided between me and Philip, with Kathleen's blessing, that I would pay for what she needed, keep receipts and then Philip would exert his power of attorney and pay me from Kathleen's account. To begin with I simply withdrew cash for her, filling her purse with the same amount she had been used to, and we continued to shop together. Gradually, though, she lost confidence at till points and I began to pay for her shopping with my debit card, removing Kathleen's involvement in any part of the transaction. Eventually, Philip oversaw all her finances whilst I bought necessities and delivered them to Kathleen. She retained ten pounds cash in her purse, 'just in case.'

Loss of cognitive capacity is measurable by decreasing competencies in the business of everyday life. Alzheimer's marks off those things that a person with dementia can no longer do without help. It demands constant adaptation to ever-changing needs.

Kathleen was blessed to have Philip assume willing responsibility for her accounts, her savings, her pension and, later, her care home costs. Loneliness and isolation have been recognised as a sad reality of modern life with many elderly people left vulnerable and alone.[6] Philip loved his aunt and was happy to afford her the protection that power of attorney gave to Kathleen. But a story of people is rarely so simple, and he had his own elderly parents and two other maiden aunts to advocate for – that is a lot to ask. Kathleen lived

---

6. National Institute on Aging, 'Social Isolation, Loneliness in Older People Pose Health Risks.'

over a hundred miles away from her nephew and he couldn't be involved in the minutiae of everyday. Financial governance is more than investment decisions and paying bills; it is the ability to get cash, buy groceries, clothes and shoes. Those with Alzheimer's at anything beyond its pre-clinical or early phases are unlikely to be able to cope well with these myriad demands. Alzheimer's disease requires those with cognitive decline to have advocates as well as friends, and, sometimes, even that is not enough.

I knew that Kathleen's time in her beloved bungalow was likely to be limited when I received a call from her on my mobile. This was deeply unusual. Despite the list of phone contacts stuck to the kitchen counter next to her telephone, she only ever dialled the familiar landline numbers. Kathleen expressed wonder at the 'phone in my pocket,' amazed that I could show her photographs and receive calls and messages. It was not dementia that left her baffled by such technology, it was simply age. She had never entered the digital world, stopping at the switch from LPs to CDs.

Although Kathleen rarely called people for chats anymore, she still used the phone to check up on arrangements. She used it when she was in a fluster, calling me or Philip for reassurance, but she had never fathomed that mobile numbers meant that she could reach us anytime.

I was on a course in London when her name flashed up on my screen as a missed call. My part-time teaching post was at a school five minutes from Kathleen's house – on any other day, I could have come straight over. But I was in the capital and my phone had been on silent during the conference. It wasn't until the coffee break that I found a fractured voicemail from Kathleen, who obviously thought my answerphone greeting had been me in real time. Clearly confused, she said that the gas man was here to read her meter and he was telling her that she needed a new burglar alarm. What should she do? Her questions were breathless and uncertain – her tone showed that whilst she recognised something was amiss in what the 'gas man' was saying to her, she no longer had the confidence and authority to respond appropriately. This was recorded proof of her lack of capacity, proof of the failing battle between Kathleen and her neuronal short circuitry. There was a pause where she expected me to speak, to advise, to calm her frenzied thoughts. She tried again, 'Karen?' trailing off when it was clear I wasn't replying. I felt sick. Someone was exploiting my friend and I wasn't there.

It was too late when I rang her back. Whether by minutes or hours, I never knew. Worried that the salesperson might have inveigled their way into her home, I first checked whether there was anyone with her. There wasn't. Kathleen said she was on her own, she wasn't expecting any visitors. She had no recollection of ringing me, no recollection of a gas man, and everything was fine. To Kathleen, it was business as usual. She was amused by my concern and urged me to enjoy my course. She would see me later.

When I arrived, there was a spanking new burglar alarm attached to the side of Kathleen's house. The gnawing worry I had been feeling all day formed a fist in my stomach. It was clear someone had ignored the 'No hawkers' sign Kathleen had put up in her better years, and taken advantage. She already had an alarm system, ironically one that was no longer used because she had forgotten all about it. She certainly didn't need an upgrade.

I went in, greeting her with my usual cheeriness. Kathleen was fine.

'Hello my dear, how lovely to see you. This is a surprise!'

Looking at me on the doorstep, she checked herself.

'Did I know you were coming?'

'It's not in the diary, don't worry,' I reassured her. 'I just pop in most days on my way home from work. I'm later today because I've been in London on a training course.'

'Ooh, lucky you. I used to like training days.'

We chatted about my day as I filled the kettle and looked around me. Sensors had appeared in the corner of the kitchen, the lounge and the dining area. My stomach felt heavy as Kathleen poured the tea.

'Can I have a quick look in your handbag, Kathleen?'

'Of course, my dear.'

She didn't even ask me why. I sat down at her dining table, pushing the post to one side, post which she now left for me to sort so that she wouldn't fall prey to charity letters and advertisements that might persuade her to write a cheque or consider setting up a direct debit. Though I was pretty certain that Kathleen could no longer follow the steps required for the latter, I knew how attached she was to her cheque book.

Opening the bag, I took out the thumbed red leather book, flicking through until I found a new stub dated that day. Printed in Kathleen's increasingly shaky handwriting was a four-figure sum.

The dread that I had struggled to keep in abeyance all day, took hold of me with physical force. I dropped my head to my chest and breathed. In. Out. Repeat. With all we had put in place to protect her, we had failed. I felt I had let her down.

Somehow, I drank tea and ate biscuits in Kathleen's lounge. Somehow, I stayed chirpy and bright and made sure she had a sandwich for later. As soon as I got home, I rang Philip. He batted away my apologies, recognising that none of us could be with Kathleen all the time. His voice remained calm and he reassured me that he was confident in his ability to sort this out. He had a battery of ammunition at his disposal – that of harnessing his power of attorney, a deeply righteous anger and his best bank manager acumen to take on the firm who had supplied the system.

Within weeks, and against all expectation, he was able to retrieve the money and have the equipment removed.

He made sure he was in the house when the company came to take everything away. They had a policy for dealing with vulnerable clients, they said. They were supposed to gain telephone consent from a relative. They had seen her list of numbers in the kitchen, tried to call several of them, but no one had replied. Kathleen had invited them in, insisted she wanted the system. They were very sorry; they had not realised the extent of her memory loss.

Kathleen's ability to respond in conversation was still good. The scenario they reported was not implausible.

This story makes me strangely grateful for Alzheimer's. Though cognitive deficit had robbed her of the template for dealing with the salesman, it also ensured that Kathleen did not remember the visit, her confusion about it, nor the installation. Philip and I never once referred to the expense she had agreed to. There was no benefit to be gained from gentle reminders not to open the door to strangers – she would not remember the advice.

Loss of short-term memory has some benefits. It makes dwelling on cross words or foolish acts impossible. It makes guilt less likely. It makes regret almost impossible. The same disease that had made Kathleen vulnerable also protected her from the shame of knowing she had signed an unnecessary cheque which constituted a significant portion of her savings. Before their removal, she occasionally commented on the new-fangled bits and bobs in her house, but not with any anxiety. When this happened, I would say that she had bought them to keep herself safe, and she was content with the sagacity of her decision. She never realised the extent to which she was taken advantage of.

Handing over financial responsibility to Philip took Kathleen months to fully understand. Following the alarm incident, Philip explained that it was time for him to take over, to put into practice the trust she had had the foresight to realise that she might one day need. He went back to the Midlands with Kathleen's cheque book in his bag. For a long time afterwards, she continued to worry about her cash book, fearful that the balances didn't tally. She missed her bank statements and was often anxious about the absence of her cheque book. She experienced sudden panics about its loss and would ring either Philip or me on repeat until her mind became distracted enough by something else to let go of the anxiety.

We didn't mind the phone calls, but we knew we had to do something to alleviate the distress she felt when we weren't on hand to reassure her. A simple note in her purse was our solution. *Philip has my cheque book and my cash book. He now looks after my money for me, so that I don't have to worry.* It wasn't in her own handwriting, but the use of the first-person was intentional and necessary.

The paper became thin with handling. I saw her read it many times, and can only guess how often she looked at it when on her own, seized with sudden concern that she had mislaid the red leather book.

Kathleen's first response to the note was merely a wry smile and a fond recollection of the nephews who loved her enough to do this for her. The second reaction was different, one that acknowledged the pain of her own detriment.

'I used to be efficient. I used to know everything about my own affairs. I wrote everything down. Now I can't remember anything at all.'

The alarm incident left a deep impression on Kathleen's family. It marked a lack of capacity in her that we had all been reluctant to see. I remained unwilling to see that she could no longer live safely on her own. I could be more vigilant. I would do more. She was still walking for her paper, deciding things for herself. She was perfectly capable of the basic activities of daily living – dressing, personal hygiene, eating – as long as I supervised the shopping and checked she was eating enough. She wasn't ready to be institutionalised; she wasn't ready for life in a wing chair and loud television. I wished

I was her daughter, that I could stop this steamroller of a decision that would change Kathleen's life for ever.

Philip and Matthew, living a distance away and being responsible for her finances, saw the situation more clearly. Their aunt was vulnerable, I couldn't be expected to be on call twenty-four hours. Friendships have limits. Depending on me was no longer practical. In their eyes, it was no longer moral – they were protecting me as much as Kathleen. They needed to do the right thing.

Kathleen, who had taken out insurance against the need to go into a residential home, who had set up the power of attorney with her nephews when she was still in her fifties and who had refitted her bathroom for a future that never transpired, was undoubtedly a practical and pragmatic person. They felt certain that she would, if she had been fully able to make the decision herself, be resolute in making the move now. They drew on a lifetime of relationship with their aunt that I didn't have, to make the best decision on her behalf, a decision they were certain she would have endorsed. It would mean that I had more free time; she would never want to become a burden on me. It would be better to do it whilst she still had some capacity to grasp the rationality behind such a move.

Amidst the resounding clamour of reason, I had no choice but to accept the decision. It was another moment for me to weep.

8
Consenting to Move

Advocacy and consent are tricky areas to negotiate when a person you love has Alzheimer's disease. For many years, much of the qualitative evidence for life management and competency in activities of daily living was provided by relatives and close friends of the person diagnosed with Alzheimer's. This primary dependence on information from carers marginalised the person living with dementia. Indeed, diagnosis still almost always includes testimony from a caregiver.[1] This remains a shifting area of concern, with increasingly effective calls for the need to understand the experience of living with dementia from the point of view of the person who has the disease rather than through proxy reports.[2] In the successful novel and film adaptation of *Still Alice*, it is only Alice's daughter who dares to ask her mother the question, 'Mom, what does it feel like? [...] Having Alzheimer's?'[3]

Care and medical supervision of people living with dementia are now firmly aligned with the concept of retaining personhood throughout the disease. Every experience of dementia is a unique one, and good practitioners and carers now recognise the importance of trying to understand what the person with dementia is feeling,

---

1. Waldemar and Burns, *Alzheimer's Disease*, 3.
2. Wilkinson, *The Perspectives of People with Dementia: Research Methods and Motivations*, 10.
3. Genova, *Still Alice*, 180.

even if they cannot fully articulate it.[4] Testimony to this is the fact that the language surrounding dementia is changing – the term senile is now rarely heard and it is more common to try to see the person first, rather than the disease – thus a *person living with dementia* rather than *Alzheimer's patient*. The shift is subtle, but enough to see that the latter use of language puts the disease first and then reduces the person to a patient, suggesting passivity and total lack of autonomy.

Carers are hugely significant in helping professionals understand the person they are caring for. Kathleen experienced good days and bad days throughout the progression of the disease, and it became necessary for me to be able to distinguish one from the other. If she was very anxious, it was symptomatic of a bad day; she wouldn't be able to express this in terms of her Alzheimer's, but she would frame her feelings by questioning her capabilities.

'I don't know what's wrong with me today; nothing seems quite right.'

This has been described as succumbing to 'sporadic episodes of confusion' which vary in length and intensity.[5] It wasn't until after Kathleen's death that I read more widely about the experiences of living with Alzheimer's. Although I had worked out a link between Kathleen's anxiety and bad days, I never fully appreciated how quickly the fog could descend and how scary or unpredictable those feelings of flailing around in ordinary life could be. Acknowledging this, it is clear that on days when confusion is less prevalent, those with the disease remain capable of fully articulating their experience. Ensuring that those living with dementia are given dignity and a voice through the confusion is key to a better understanding of their experience and their needs.

Whilst focus on personhood and continuing autonomy is absolutely right, it is arguably predicated on a pre-existing relationship. To understand Kathleen with dementia necessitated understanding who Kathleen was prior to cognitive impairment. In many ways, the retaining of individuality is based on love.

Philip and Matthew, together with Terence, loved Kathleen. In deciding the time was right to start looking for a care home, they

---

4. Williamson, *Older People's Mental Health Today*, 74.

5. Wilkinson, *The Perspectives of People with Dementia: Research Methods and Motivations*, 106.

factored in Kathleen's personality, character and experience. They understood her pragmatism and acknowledged that she would want to retain independence to the end, relying not on wider family and risking becoming a burden but preferring to fund her own care in an establishment that had been deeply considered and well-chosen. They recognised that provision of a nursing home would be a means to extend her independence, ensuring that her wider family would not be encumbered by worries about her care.

They were not wrong in this. Even during the more advanced stages of the disease, Kathleen remained thoughtful. She never wanted to put the nursing staff to any trouble, and she regularly reminded me,

'I don't want to be a burden on you. You have your family to consider.'

Kathleen loved my family and they loved her. This remained a fact even though towards the end of her life, she had forgotten their names. She had forgotten Emily had got married and that James was at university. When she saw a photograph of my daughter's wedding, it was poignantly clear that she had no memory of what they looked like, mistaking the groom as my son, and my daughter, Emily, as the new addition to the family.

'Has she fitted in well with you all?' she asked me.

This moment caught me completely off-guard. I fought back tears as I turned the conversation to the beautiful dress and the blessings of the day.

Kathleen may have heartbreakingly forgotten names and details, but she never once forgot their existence. Bound up in her knowledge of me was the certainty of family. I had a family who needed me, and Kathleen never wanted her needs to usurp theirs.

Gaining meaningful consent from a person living with dementia is fraught with difficulty. Kathleen was able to understand complex concepts in the space of a brief conversation, her working memory allowing a thirty second window of comprehension, but then all content would vanish, evidence of her anterograde memory losses. Philip spoke to Kathleen throughout the process of finding and selecting a residential home, but she was never fully aware of the enormity or the practical implications of the decision that was largely being made on her behalf. During each conversation, however, it was clear that Kathleen held strong views about remaining local. We pointed out that a move to the Midlands would mean easy access both to Philip and her brother, Terence, but her reply was always the same.

'I have lived in Maidenhead all my adult life. My friends are here, my church is here. I cannot imagine being anywhere else.'

Despite the fact that she was already refusing lifts to church, giving reasons such as being tired or feeling ill in order to avoid the clamour of people and the possibility of embarrassment when she might fail to recognise someone she had known for decades; despite the fact that the teas with colleagues were tailing off and she no longer wanted to visit her friends, her identity remained firmly rooted in what she had always done, in where she had always lived. If I gently reminded her that she found the Sunday services too much and hadn't been for some months, she would be astonished.

'What do you mean? I go every week.'

Or,

'I haven't been. Has it come to that already?'

I learnt to go along with Kathleen's version of herself, the script that had been forged over a period of more than fifty years was not going to be immediately overwritten by Alzheimer's. She recognised that she had some failure in recall but had not computed the extent of the deficit.[6] If it contented her to believe that she still went to church regularly, then so be it. I never lied to her, but I didn't always correct her assumptions – if her memory had rooted in something she had done weeks, months or even years before, then it seemed more loving to let it stand.

With power of attorney in place, it was technically her nephews' decision to sell Kathleen's house and make the move into a care home. Philip and Matthew toured numerous local residential facilities before coming up with a shortlist of three or four. They took their aunt with them once they had made the final cull. I didn't go on these visits, but Philip reported that Kathleen had declared one 'too much like a school' and she didn't want to spend her twilight years in a place with wide corridors that reminded her of work. Another seemed too small and 'perhaps a little close to the river.' The geography teacher in her remained wise to flood plains and consequent risk.

Their regard for her personhood, for her involvement in the decision was exemplary. Philip took photos of each home and

---

6. Segal, Qualls and Smyer, *Aging and Mental Health*, 187.

printed them on A4 paper, labelled with their names and locations. He left them on Kathleen's coffee table where I could pick them up and invite conversation about them.

'This one looks nice.'

'Possibly, my dear, but too dark for me.'

'I can imagine you in a room like this.'

'Yes. I like the views too. Look at all the trees.'

Our conversations were relevant, but never fully invested in the fact that Kathleen might soon be moving away from her bungalow and moving into residential care. She was able to evaluate each house by its photographs, discuss which she preferred, but on a cerebral rather than a practical level. Her world was reducing to the present and the remote past. The recent past and the ability to plan ahead and visualise a future was already deeply impaired. This meant that the final decision to move rested with Philip and Matthew. Their fear over her vulnerability, revealed starkly in the episode over the burglar alarm, had convinced them that a care facility was the only viable option to keep Kathleen safe.

The Mental Capacity Act 2005 provides a framework in England and Wales for assessing capacity and for making decisions on behalf of those who are deemed to lack it.[7] Recognising that Kathleen had already made an unwise financial decision that had the potential to derail her savings, both nephews agreed that it was time to exert their power of attorney over Kathleen's continuing care.

The Mental Capacity Act divides decisions into those which are less complex and others which are deemed to be more complex.[8] It was apparent that Kathleen was still able, with support, to deal effectively with less complex decision-making. Given a choice of meals, she could select one with little difficulty; she chose her own clothes each day and she was still making the choice to walk every day to get her paper. The more complex decisions such as where to live, and when and if to spend large sums of money were more compromised.

Despite this, Kathleen was always part of the process. Even if she couldn't fully connect the fact that looking at care homes and photographs equated to her moving out of her bungalow and

7. Alzheimer's Society's, 'Alzheimer's Society's View on Decision Making.'

8. Graham and Cowley, *A Practical Guide to the Mental Capacity Act 2005*, 134, 135.

surrendering a significant amount of independence, Philip and Matthew ensured that her needs and wishes remained central. They were making the decision in her best interests, eschewing the perhaps more practical path of moving Kathleen nearer to Philip, because she was still very able to express her preference for staying in the south-east. The Code of Practice states that the wishes and feelings of the person who lacks capacity can be demonstrated orally, in writing, through behaviour or habits and through emotional reaction and expressions of pleasure or distress, and that they must be taken into account when decisions are made.[9] Philip and Matthew were intuitively following this code.

It was evident that everything was being done to support Kathleen in this transition from independence to assisted living. Having established the plausibility of all the homes on the shortlist, the final decision was taken by Kathleen. Together we studied the photographs of the care homes and she consistently selected one home above the others over a period of weeks. It was the same one that 'the boys' had liked, and so it was duly chosen, and her name put on the waiting list. I made sure that we talked about it frequently, making Bluebell House a normal topic of conversation, willing the whole idea of a move to stick in the fractured communication networks of her brain.

The first vacancy to be offered came quickly – too quickly for me. I needed more time to get used to the idea and was struggling to envisage visiting Kathleen in a more formal environment, struggling with the losses it might impose on our relationship. Kathleen was offered a room on the top floor of this rather grand Victorian mansion house.

Philip invited me to accompany them this time. I was eager to see where Kathleen might soon be living but was also aware of the tenuous position of being friend rather than family. It was not my place to offer opinion. I knew Matthew hardly at all, and Philip rather better, but, even so, we had little shared history beyond the diagnosis of Kathleen's Alzheimer's. Our conversations were polite and the trust between us too new to be tested. I planned to stay very quiet.

The room was in the eaves and had a romantic sloping ceiling with portholes to view the garden. Philip and Matthew were

---

9.   Graham and Cowley, *A Practical Guide to the Mental Capacity Act 2005*, 136.

impressed. It was clean, respectable and with distinct areas for sleeping and sitting.

'You could have friends here. This sitting section is lovely.'

Kathleen seemed to understand what was being asked of her – could she live here? I sensed tension between her nephews' eagerness to get their aunt into a safe place as soon as possible, and Kathleen's unease as she tried valiantly to list favourable aspects of the attic space.

'The lounge is nice. The porthole windows are fun. And I like the separate area.'

I cannot know what was in her head as she inspected the room and responded to her nephews. I knew that she valued them highly and wouldn't want to disappoint them with her response. I saw my friend trying her best to give the answer hoped for and expected of her. Maybe they saw something more positive.

Kathleen rightly trusted Philip and Matthew to help her make an efficacious decision. As we all stooped to accommodate the sloping roof, no one could get away from the fact that an eaves room was probably not the best choice for a woman of 5 ft 10. To see out of the circular windows, you needed to be seated or bent over. I plucked up the courage to speak. Drawing Philip to one side I asked whether I might put a spanner in the works. He nodded and then listened as I admitted that I didn't think this room was right, that I would rather care for her a bit longer in her own home, wait for a better option. This one was too compact, too big a compromise on light and comfort.

It wasn't that I was trying to stop the move. At least I don't think it was. I recognised the greater wisdom of Philip and Matthew who shared decades of love for their aunt. Intuitively, I knew they were more likely to know what was right for Kathleen at this point in her life. But this wasn't the right room.

Although Philip agreed with me, his anxiety at leaving her in her own home was doing battle with the impracticality of the attic room. He wanted her safely out of the way of salespeople and scammers. He wanted her medical needs provided for. Perhaps this would do to start with, until another room became vacant?

The care home manager sensed our conflicting emotions,

'We do have another bedroom you can look at,' she explained. 'It's usually used for short stays, respite care, but you're welcome to consider it.'

She turned to Kathleen.

'You are rather tall.'

'Yes. This might be a little difficult for me,' Kathleen acknowledged.

We followed the manager down a set of stairs, out of the eaves and onto the first floor. In the corner was a dual aspect room, with full-height ceiling and large windows. It had a totally different feel. Kathleen looked at the space along a sunlit wall,

'My piano could go here.' She exclaimed. 'I am allowed my piano, aren't I?'

'You certainly are. We'd be delighted to be entertained by you, Kathleen,' the matron replied with warmth.

The four of us crowded around the doorway as Kathleen sashayed from window to window to compare the views.

'I can see the car park. I like that. I will be able to watch all the comings and goings from my chair.'

She was already using possessive pronouns – something had happened, and Kathleen had moved in. She understood, in that moment, what was being planned, and she was central to the decision. She was, in the words of the Mental Capacity Act 2005, clearly expressing pleasure and positive emotions.[10] Looking across at Philip, we shared a complicit smile. He had found the right place for his aunt and everyone was happy.

---

10.   Graham and Cowley, *A Practical Guide to the Mental Capacity Act 2005*, 136.

9
Groundhog Day

Apart from a brief spell when her ailing mother came to live with her, Kathleen lived alone for all her adult life. Consequently, she had accumulated a lifetime of possessions uncurated by anyone else. She owned a library of books, tapes, CDs, and box upon box of sheet music. All this needed to be sorted out so that Philip and Matthew would know which things were moving with her to Bluebell House and which were being left at the bungalow.

Deciding how to negotiate the logistics of a house move is challenging at the best of times – it is even more so when you are doing it with someone who is living with dementia. Although I was as confident as I could be that Kathleen had consented to the move, I was pretty sure that she lacked the ability to plan for it. Her past was built on shifting sands, some days accessible, others not. Her short-term memory was very poor, and she could articulate no recollection of visiting the homes or choosing her room. Comprehending that she was going to leave her bungalow, the one she could still confidently tell me that she had bought off-plan when the new estate went up in the 1980s, was impossible. Alzheimer's makes the past unreliable and the future inconceivable, and whilst there is some freedom in living always for the moment, it made it very hard for us to prepare Kathleen for the move.

That we are much more than our memories can be seen in the emotional reactions of those with dementia. Despite the neuronal atrophy associated with Alzheimer's, experience has shown that most people with cognitive impairment have continuing ability to show emotion, respond to others and retain emotional memory.[1] I knew that if I were to leave my home with little real choice, I would feel anxious and sad. I worried that Kathleen's lack of understanding about the impending move would heighten her emotional responses on the day of the move. I had seen a very emotional side to her after diagnosis and again when she reacted badly to the *donepezil*, and I didn't want her to be hurt, confused or distressed when she left her bungalow.

Kathleen could no longer prepare herself for such a change; she couldn't arm herself with the sort of stoicism I might employ in order to cope with something I was dreading. All I could do was keep talking about it calmly and positively, and hope that somewhere in her brain there were enough working neurotransmitters to make the fact stick.

There weren't. Acetylcholine is a neurotransmitter that should be distributed throughout the brain; in Alzheimer's it is thought that a lack of this organic chemical in certain regions of the brain is responsible for key aspects of lost memory function.[2] Even on a good day, Kathleen was no longer retaining her immediate yesterdays. She could be very involved in a conversation about the move but have no real grasp of the context as it applied to her. This was made very clear during our efforts to sort the bungalow. A sense of humour was required as we made our first attempt to sort through a lifetime of clothes. Kathleen had fully utilised wardrobes in two of her three bedrooms and owned more coats than I imagined possible for a single human being.

'So, we have a navy mackintosh and an identical one in beige.'

'Yes. I often buy different colours of the same thing. When you find something that suits you, it makes sense.'

It does indeed. This habit is another quirky similarity between us; my daughter teases me often over my purchases. *You've bought a new jumper. Nice. How many colours did you get?*

---

1. Karger, 'Emotional Experience in Patients with Advanced Alzheimer's Disease from the Perspective of Families, Professional Caregivers, Physicians, and Scientists,' 316.

2. 'The Brain from the Top to the Bottom.'

'I understand. But you've also got a wax jacket, a formal wool coat, a green cagoule, a gilet, and several long blazers. Oh, and here's the famous sheepskin!'

'I can't get rid of that. It is invaluable in the snow. I've had it for years.'

'Well, you aren't going to have room in a single wardrobe for ten coats,' I pointed out, trying to appeal to her pragmatism. 'Some of them will have to go.'

'But they're all useful. I wear them all.'

Kathleen's tone brokered no compromise. I knew I needed to keep the mood light and positive, and I had certainly never seen most of these coats off their hangers.

'Really?' I smiled at her, raising my eyebrows quizzically.

'Yes.'

Kathleen could be stubborn, and she certainly never threw anything away before its time. This was not symptomatic of dementia, but an intrinsic part of her character. A teenager in the war, rationing had given her a lifelong habit of reuse and recycle long before it became a modern mantra. The profusion of notes around her bungalow were written on the backs of envelopes. Scrap paper was held together with giant paperclips to form mini notebooks. Nothing was wasted. Trying to encourage Kathleen to consider donating 'perfectly good clothes' to a charity shop was a non-starter.

'They still fit. I wear them. Why would I give them away?'

'Because the room you are moving into has only one small wardrobe.' I lifted my tone to turn the statement into a question.

'That is a problem,' she conceded.

'Shall we decide which coats you wear the most and donate the others to charity?'

'But they still fit. I wear them all. Why would I give them away?'

Such circular conversations were getting us nowhere and despite the fact that we were still laughing, it was clear to me that anxiety and frustration were waiting in the wings to besiege us both. Tea and biscuits were called for.

Applying normal logic to a situation is not sufficient when one of you has Alzheimer's. There is no point in becoming agitated. Fortunately, I am blessed with a reasonably placid, non-confrontational personality and so staying calm does not usually present a difficulty for me. Friends whose parents had dementia felt the battle with anger and frustration more deeply. I believe this is because something guttural was changing for them, as they witnessed a form of deconstruction of the parent they had always known and depended upon. Kathleen was my friend; had never been my parental figure. I suppose, even before Alzheimer's, I had been a facilitator for her, taking her to Bible study when she no longer wanted to drive in the dark, becoming a friendly taxi when she wanted to give up driving altogether. Looking back, I was an intrinsic part of her ageing process.

The break in activity halted Kathleen's looping thought process and provided me with space to think of an alternative approach. I came up with a cunning plan. Kathleen's-trunk-in-Karen's-attic was the solution. The two most useful coats would be afforded space in the cupboard at Bluebell House and I would hold all the others in reserve, becoming her wardrobe mistress for a special occasion or a change of season. No need to get rid of any and no problem with storage. With Kathleen's approval for this idea, I carted several armfuls to my car before she could change her mind. Out of sight really is out of mind when decluttering the house of a person with Alzheimer's.

The coat process was repeated for polo-neck jumpers – about fifteen of them, in varying shades of beige, blue and green – then skirts, trousers, blouses, vests and all the sundries gathering dust in the lavender-scented drawers and shelves of Kathleen's clothes collection.

I knew from previous expeditions to buy new trousers in ever-decreasing sizes, that Kathleen had a clothes quirk that I'm pretty certain pre-dated Alzheimer's. As I never shopped with her for clothing prior to her diagnosis, I cannot be sure, but it seemed to be a hard-wired habit that she found as sensible as I found astonishing. When I was a little girl, my mum made me wear a petticoat whenever I wore a skirt. A cross between a vest and a slip, I ditched them as soon as I was old enough to dress myself, but Kathleen loved them. Used to wearing skirts each day at work, this love wasn't misplaced, but at her retirement she switched from formal skirt suits to a penchant for trousers. Now, she always wore trousers.

In a changing room in Marks and Spencer's I discovered that she also always wore a petticoat. She popped it over her head and tucked the vast expanse of slip into the waistband of her trousers, thus acquiring the appearance of a much larger woman.

In sort-mode, I wondered if I dared to cull the petticoat collection.

'We can get rid of most of these slips,' I suggested. 'You never wear skirts, so you won't need them.'

'I need to keep all the skirts. What if there is a special dinner? Or an event? I'll need to be smart then.'

We laughed. She seemed to realise that our agendas were slightly conflicted and took joy in tussling over the packing. Unlike Kathleen, I am a declutterer – anything unused for six months is easy prey for charity shop fodder in my house. On some level, Kathleen appeared to relish being stubborn, and delight in the mild exasperation that I am sure was beginning to show on my face. Alzheimer's may have robbed her short-term memory, may have rendered her no longer capable of managing some of the activities of daily living without support, but it had not put out the twinkle of mischief that characterised Kathleen right to the end. She was most definitely still there. With dementia, it is all too easy to count the detriments; we were learning to celebrate what remained.

And with that comment, I saw a glimmer of hope that Kathleen still retained some capacity for medium-term recall. She had, almost without my noticing it, made a statement with regard to her future. *What if there is a special dinner? Or an event?* She was voicing understanding of where she was going. She had expectations of something good, something enriching. She wasn't troubled about the move at all.

With good humour and further cups of tea I conceded to all her clothing decisions, unknowingly putting into practice Principle 3 of the Mental Capacity Act – to accept Kathleen's ability to make decisions even if I thought better ones could have been made.[3]

All the skirts and petticoats were packed, folded into tissue and kept pristine for those occasions she might just need to look smart. We utilised every spare nook and cranny in the suitcase. The same suitcase that had taken Kathleen round the world in 1984.

Once we had waged war with the clothes, we needed to decide on the trinkets, the stationery, the personal belongings that Kathleen wanted to surround herself with. Several times she wandered through the bungalow and returned, presenting me with a saucepan or a kettle in order that it could be stowed away with everything else.

'No. You won't need those – Bluebell House are going to do all your cooking.'

---

3. Graham and Cowley, *A Practical Guide to the Mental Capacity Act 2005*, 53.

'All my cooking?' The stress on the first word highlighted her astonishment.

'Yes. You won't have to worry about that anymore. Someone will make your lunch and serve it to you.'

She looked perturbed. Perhaps she understood less than I had hoped. Kathleen didn't grasp the full context of the move. And it didn't take much for my own worries to resurface – that life in a nursing home would be a backward step for my friend. Any independence she had managed to retain since her diagnosis seemed to be slipping away. I could see this, but she couldn't really fathom it. Philip and Matthew were protected by distance and a strong sense that this was the only option. Any doubts I still harboured were doubts that I couldn't share. Swallowing down a creeping sense of dread, I tried a remote memory in an attempt to connect Kathleen's past to this new vision of the present.

'Did you cook for yourself at university?'

'No, my dear. All meals were served in the dining hall. I got very fat!'

I laughed out loud. I could not imagine a fat Kathleen.

'I did,' she insisted. 'Three meals a day and all cooked.'

'And that's what you'll be getting at Bluebell House.'

'I suppose it is,' she said, her anxiety subdued for now.

Which personal belongings to pack was the trickiest to decide. A cuddly tiger who had resided on her hearth for decades was popped in the box first. Kathleen's thimble collection, though numerous, was a plausible contender – she had a mantelshelf in her new room, and they could fill that, alongside a set of cranberry glassware and a porcelain figure. These were wrapped in tissue and carefully placed in the box. Her stationery items were testimony to a lifetime in teaching. Who can resist the lure of a new pen and notebook? Unable to conceive of a life where she wouldn't need to file receipts and spend hours on home admin, we packed Sellotape, Blu Tack, paper clips, drawing pins, envelopes, file paper, coloured pencils, biros, staplers, staples, highlighters and sticky labels. We packed Tippex and rulers and compasses, sharpeners and a pair of china wellington boots to hold desk pencils. And then I labelled the outside of the box and sealed it, adding to the increasing wall of cardboard in the lounge.

We packed soap and flannels, toothbrush and paste, shampoo and face cream. We packed lipstick and perfume, combs and brushes,

tissues and toilet roll. We packed shoes and boots and sandals and slippers. Dressing gowns – four of them, all different weights –
'I need all those. What if one is in the wash, my dear?'
We packed nighties, bed-socks and enough pairs of tights to open a hosiery business, and I labelled and stuck down the boxes.

Rewarding ourselves with Kathleen's favourite treat of Thornton's millionaire shortbread bites, we sank back in her Ercol chairs and sat quietly.

'What are all those boxes for?' she asked.

I took her hand and explained once more that she was moving to a lovely house which Philip and Matthew had found and that she had loved.

'Have I been there, then?'

'You have indeed. I'll move the boxes to the spare room where they won't bother you so much. We're all ready now.'

After heating some macaroni cheese and leaving her eating at the dining table, I went home. Tomorrow we would tackle the books.

The next day I rang the doorbell with some trepidation. Moving was scheduled for the end of the week. Much of the packing was completed, but it felt like there was still a lot to do. Looking back, I see that I wanted everything to be ready for Philip's arrival, a proof that Kathleen and I were a team, that we could manage life and all Alzheimer's could throw at us. In some unacknowledged way, I was trying to prove the fact of the move unnecessary.

Despite the early hour, Kathleen was up, dressed and cheerful.

'Good morning. All set for more packing?' I asked.

'Certainly. I've been busy already.'

This was hopeful. My worry meter oscillated to a positive swing once more as I wondered whether Kathleen had managed to make a connection between the suitcases, the boxes and her impending move. Perhaps the wrench of leaving her home could be managed well after all.

I followed her into the hall. A pile of vests on the floor by the airing cupboard were testimony to Kathleen's busyness. Vests we had neatly packed the day before. Steering Kathleen into what had been a firmly shut spare room, the now wide-open door revealed that every case and box we had filled in the previous days had been opened and the contents scattered.

'I'm doing very well,' Kathleen announced proudly.

'You are indeed,' a slightly hysterical laugh escaped my lips. 'What is it you're actually doing?'

'I found all these boxes and cases this morning. I'm enjoying sorting them out and putting everything into its right place.'

'That's great,' I said, keeping my voice bright and arranging my face to match her obvious pleasure.

My Alzheimer's learning curve got a little steeper as I contemplated how to play this one. I had thought my system foolproof – everything had been precisely labelled so that I could reassure Kathleen that all the important things had been packed. Notes had been our way of making sense of the everyday for a long time, and until now they had pretty much worked. I had assumed we were creating a ready-reference guide to make the packing and removals process easier. But it was clear that she had forgotten all about Bluebell House. It was also clear that she had been at it since the early hours, testimony to a disturbed sleep pattern common in dementia.[4] Finding this treasure trove in her spare room had given her hours of pleasure.

Any thought of tackling the books was abandoned. Checking her sink and waste basket in the kitchen, it appeared that breakfast hadn't happened that morning. I put the kettle on, and we sat in a lounge that still looked like Kathleen's. She wasn't going to take much furniture with her to Bluebell House, so that was all in its rightful places. The coffee table was still spread with customary magazines and the bookcases were, of course, still full.

I placed a bowl of cereal on her dining table and we sat in companionable silence as she ate her breakfast and sipped a hot cup of coffee. The only evidence of the imminent house move in this part of the bungalow was the absence of tiger and Kathleen's thimbles.

'You're off on an adventure soon,' I began.

'I am?'

'Yes. We need to pack some boxes of clothes and things for you to move to Bluebell House.'

'Am I moving?'

'You are indeed. To a lovely house with views. There are people there to look after you whenever you might need it. I'm going to let you finish your coffee whilst I have a look at some of the packing in the spare room. You've made a good start on it yourself.' I pushed the

---

4. Moe et al., 'Sleep/Wake Patterns in Alzheimer's Disease,' 15.

crossword across the table. 'You relax now and finish your breakfast. Do the crossword, if you like. I'll be in the spare room when you want to join me.'

'Thank you, dear,' she beamed.

I scurried around the house, repacking items and not worrying too much if the carefully written labels now belied the contents of the boxes and cases. I used liberal Sellotape to seal them down and managed to restore some order before Kathleen joined me.

'Let's just keep this door closed. We're all ready.'

'Remind me what we're ready for …'

This cycle went on in some form for several days, though I had at least learnt to secrete some of the boxes in my car to prevent nocturnal unpacking. When Philip arrived to stay the night before the move, a slightly more harassed version of Karen greeted him at Kathleen's front door. I gave him a potted history of the week and warned him of possible night-time activity.

'It had to be seen to be believed,' he said the following morning. 'Nothing I could say would persuade her that she had enough clothes in her drawers to last her until the move. I've spent most of this morning repacking.'

His explanation suddenly shed light on Kathleen's thought processes. Of course. Why hadn't I thought of that? I was exasperated with myself for failing the empathy test. I should have thought about what Kathleen was seeing when she got up each morning. She had been opening her drawers and wardrobes and finding little there – just the right number of tops, vests and trousers she needed to see her through to move day. She hadn't computed she was moving, so all she saw was lack of choice. Even if the move day hovered on the edges of her consciousness, the calculation of time – of days left until the move – meant nothing to her at all. It was natural, therefore, that she needed to re-appropriate her clothes to the right places. It was a logical, intelligent response to the emptying drawers, just missing the crucial context that her short-term memory no longer supplied.

10
Moving On

Most people with Alzheimer's or other forms of dementia eventually need to depend, to some extent, on outside care. A study for Alzheimer's Research UK recently found that 60 per cent of those receiving home-care services are living with dementia. In care homes 69 per cent of residents have a dementia diagnosis.[1] Such a shift in independence needs careful emotional management.

Having Alzheimer's has been likened to having different bookcases in the brain. In the analogy, factual memories of places, events and people are stored in ascending order on a cheap, self-assembly shelving unit. The most recent memories, from yesterday, last week and last month are precariously balanced on the top shelf whilst memories from childhood are more carefully stored at the bottom. Alzheimer's comes and shakes the structure, dislodging recent experiences first, continuing to shake until remnants of memories are all that remain. Such a seismic shift in brain function causes anxiety and loss of confidence. These emotions are possible because there is a second bookcase. This one is sturdy and oaken and stores more abstract ideas – it is firm on the floor and has tightly packed volumes of feelings where voices of loved ones are filed, as are emotions of wellbeing, affection, security and protection. Fear is also in there, as is confusion and worry. When shaken by dementia,

---

1.   Dementia Statistics Hub, 'Care Services.'

these volumes are more resistant; tightly packed, they are less likely to fall, leaving the emotional, feeling person intact.[2]

Such evocative metaphors provided by those living with Alzheimer's emphasise how much care is needed to preserve emotional integrity. Managing Kathleen's move meant taking care of her emotional being over and above all the logistics and practicalities. She needed to feel secure and loved through the process.

Philip had devised a plan which meant that Kathleen wouldn't see the contents of her bungalow being removed. Although it was already a little bare – drawers and wardrobes much depleted of their contents – the basic layout and furnishings had not changed. The television was still in the corner opposite the armchairs. The coffee table and magazines were still in the middle of the lounge. The books had remained stubbornly on their shelves, the spines mocking my belief that I could sort everything before Philip's arrival. The kitchen hadn't been touched. By preserving the sense of home, we hoped to make the leaving of it less traumatic. When I asked friends how they managed their parents' move into care, Margaret described taking leave of her mother's home with just 'a small suitcase, as if she was going on holiday.'[3] It seems that we all try to minimise the emotional impact for those we love.

We decided that it would be best for Kathleen if I took her out for the morning. Meanwhile, her nephews would load the hired van with boxes and suitcases that had miraculously managed to stay packed. They would ensure the electric piano bought with her brother, was part of this first tranche.

It was July, the sun high and already warm when I knocked on the door to pick up my friend from her home for the last time. Philip was struggling to stay cheerful; I attempted to signal understanding through my facial expression. He nodded at me, and by some sort of mutual consent, we decided it best not to say too much or offer hugs. It was an effort for all of us to appear normal, for me to remain light-hearted and positive.

'I thought Dorney Court for coffee this morning, Kathleen,' I said.

2. Mitchell, *Somebody I Used to Know*, 97–8.
3. Martin, MH interview.

'I think we've been there before.' A tone of caution crept into her voice, as if she were testing a memory pathway but could no longer be certain of its authenticity.

'We have. It has a walled garden and a fountain. It's our favourite place for a treat.'

'Then that sounds splendid.' She looked towards Philip and Matthew. 'Are you coming with us?'

'No,' Philip laughed. 'We're going to do the hard work of moving your boxes while you two eat cake!'

'That sounds like a good plan.' Her eyes twinkled with mischief as she recognised that we were getting the better deal.

Philip and Matthew were going to take the packed items straight to Bluebell House. They were determined to set up the corner room with Kathleen's things, so that it would be immediately familiar on her arrival. My instructions were simple: keep Kathleen occupied until the message came in that everything was ready.

We left the bungalow and turned down the road, my heartbeat harder and more insistent than usual. Kathleen had closed her front door as she always did, showing no indication that she understood it would be for the last time. She checked she had her keys and her handbag and was completely happy to be taken out on such a beautiful day. I, on the other hand, was fully aware that for the first time since she had left her parents' home in 1946, she was losing her independence. She was going to live somewhere which required a code to get in and out, a code that would be impossible for her to remember. Today she had woken up in her own home, capable of walking out for her paper or catching a bus. Tomorrow she would be dependent on visitors to take her out, and her horizons would shrink. That July morning, it was me, Philip and Matthew who had to stay in control of our emotions.

A move to a care home can be more traumatic for family than for the person with Alzheimer's. Another friend found it hard to talk about, battling with necessity and guilt.

'I'd arranged for the couple of people who cared for her to come and just see her and say hi, pop in for a cup of tea. I told Mum that *They're going to come and see you, because you're going to be away for Christmas.* But I knew, they knew they were saying goodbye.'[4]

---

4. Martin, EF interview.

I wasn't saying goodbye to Kathleen; if anything the move to Bluebell House had the potential to enhance our relationship. We wouldn't have to shop and cook, we could just enjoy each other's company; but it didn't feel good. It didn't feel like an opportunity. There is something inherent in committing loved ones with dementia to the care of others that makes us uneasy. Acknowledgement that independent living is no longer safe or wise doesn't assuage the guilt that carers and family members often experience.[5] We don't want to feel relief, but acknowledge that residential care gives respite to the responsibilities we have been carrying. We don't want to feel jealous, but at the same time we are deeply reluctant to accept that others are now responsible for caring.

Kathleen had organised her finances so that she could be cared for in a residential home if the time came. Aware of her single status and determined never to burden her family emotionally or financially, administrative preparations made decades before were a clear signal of her future acquiescence to institutional care. This seems to be a self-awareness perhaps limited to those who are single. For the rest of us, there is a vague sense that we might be looked after, a security placed on family that allows us not to think of deterioration or death. Friends who have recently placed their parents into the care of residential facilities relied on past conversations. Margaret's mother had always said that, if necessary, she would go into a care home.[6] Jayne's mother had stated similar things, wanting her daughters to live full lives of their own, unencumbered by the need to care. When she could no longer keep her mother safe at a distance of over 250 miles, Jayne simply admitted,

'We cannot care for you as you need to be cared for. We have looked and found a home that we like. We think it's the best place for you and would like you to try it.'[7] Her mother's acquiescence was simple. Her eyes filmed and she just nodded.

Generously, these women all prioritised the needs of the younger generation over their own, handing over the decision to their children. Kathleen had participated fully in the process of choosing a home but living with dementia meant that she could not hold

---

5. BMC Geriatrics, 'How People with Dementia and Their Families Decide about Moving to a Care Home and Support Their Needs: Development of a Decision Aid, a Qualitative Study,' 7.

6. Martin, MH interview.

7. Martin, EF interview.

onto the salient facts. Her consent to move was wholehearted, but we were fully aware that it was made with the limiting effects of dementia. Having lost the insight to assess risk for herself, she put herself in her nephews' hands, reliant on those she loved to make the best choice for her.[8]

Any doubt we may have had over the move to Bluebell House was assuaged by Kathleen's entirely positive attitude. Pragmatic her whole life long and further proved by practical decisions made immediately after her retirement, Kathleen's core personality was stoic.

Philip had booked his aunt into the care home for a three-week trial period. This gave everyone concerned a chance to change their minds, but in reality we all knew that this was a decision unlikely to be reversed. As the days progressed, she would occasionally ask me, 'Is this where I live now?' and 'What happened to my bungalow?' I explained that Bluebell House was her new home, a place where she could be looked after. I repeated the assurance that if she didn't like it, then we could think again.

'But why would I want to leave? It's like a hotel here.'

At an emotional level, she understood she was being cared for. A self-sufficient, working woman all her life, such a feeling equated to luxury.

On that July day Kathleen simply pulled the door shut, checked her handbag and keys and joined me in the car. She enjoyed our coffee at the hideaway garden centre that nestles in the shadow of a Tudor house and has its own walled garden, vegetable patches and pond. We sat outside under the shade of trees in full summer leaf and waited for our coffee. For Kathleen, the present had become her only real point of reference and, for now at least, the present was relaxed, warm and very pleasant.

In that moment, it was only me who harboured the burden of context. I can tell you exactly where we sat: in green ironwork chairs at the front of the café. It wasn't our usual spot, but the garden tables were bleached in the glare of full sun and Kathleen wanted a cooler place to sip her strong, sugared coffee. I pushed a yoghurt-coated cranberry flapjack around my plate as Kathleen relished the challenge of her caramel shortbread. She was no different from

8.   BMC Geriatrics, 'How People with Dementia and Their Families Decide about Moving to a Care Home and Support Their Needs: Development of a Decision Aid, a Qualitative Study,' 7.

usual, insisting on cutting the toffee treat with a knife so that she could eat delicate bite-size morsels, but I felt very different. I couldn't escape the notion that I was party to a heist which would end up with Kathleen in a room where before she'd had a whole bungalow, where she would be contained when until now she had been free. I found myself incapable of staying in the moment and kept chatting about Bluebell House, attempting to create the sort of excitement I had seen Kathleen express in earlier days when she had planned holidays. It was difficult to accept that not so long ago she had booked coach tours and travelled independently, frequenting favourite places like Alnwick, a trip that involved going miles from her home.

'I'm not going home after this then?' she said, pointing at the shortbread.

'Not today. Philip and Matthew are just finishing up your packing and then they are doing the hard work of moving your bits and pieces to Bluebell House. When I get a message on my phone, we'll head over and see what they've managed to do with your new room.'

'Am I staying there?'

'Yes, for three weeks initially, then you can stay forever if you like it.'

I needn't have worried. Kathleen has never dwelt in self-pity or regret. If Philip thought she needed to be in a nursing home, then she needed to be in a nursing home. If Philip had found the home with Matthew, then it was bound to be the best place that she could afford, and she would be grateful. She would not want to be a burden on them in her old age, and she thought that she might be forgetting things more often these days.

Bluebell House is an old redbrick manor perched high on a hillside. Its terraced garden has wide patios and low walls so that all residents can enjoy the views over far-reaching fields, see the silver snaking of the Thames in the distance and the golden clock face of Cliveden Manor glinting in the summer sun. On clear days, through squinted eye, it is possible to make out Windsor Castle. On the more practical side of the house there is a gravel car park and a small courtyard adorned with pots. Over the hedge is a field dotted with sheep in the winter months but left to grass for the most part of the year. No matter the season, water trickles down Spring Lane, the access road that leads to the steep drive to Bluebell House.

As I dropped the car into first gear to negotiate the tight left turn that marks the entrance to the drive, I worried about the winters ahead. Snow would make it impossible to access the house – had they provision for that?

At the top of the hill, the tarmac drive gave way to gravel and we parked my little Aygo in a space that afforded a good view of Kathleen's new home.

'This looks just like my grammar school,' Kathleen remarked as our feet crunched on the stones.

'Your school must have been very grand then.'

'I suppose it was quite.'

'Your new home reminds me of Malory Towers,' I say, but the Enid Blyton allusion of my youth is lost on Kathleen. 'It is stunning,' I admitted, trying to regulate my voice. It sounded strangled in my own head, too high, too bright.

'It's beautiful.'

Kathleen's reply was warm and confident. I wondered how much of all this she understood.

Beyond these details, I remember nothing of actually getting us to Room 21. Sometimes traumatic or emotional memories become beacons for us, something we can't let go of or unsee. Sometimes, our brains just wash memories away, preventing us from revisiting times we found particularly hard. The physiology of this phenomenon is one of the mysteries of memory that has yet to be explained. Psychologically, it has been suggested that we are able to discard memories that impede our ability to move forward.[9] Perhaps I needed to forget my fingers tapping in the entry code for the first time, needed to lose the memory of walking through a residents' lounge full of people that neither of us knew.

Forgetting is as important as remembering in our quest to be ourselves. We gloss over histories that we'd rather bury, and we lose detail as years and events merge in the flotsam and jetsam of our past. This is something that is not dwelt upon in the consideration of dementia. We all forget. None of us has a full biography, and yet those with Alzheimer's are still regarded with a level of caution. Reaction to those living with Alzheimer's is compromised – it is easy to lose sight of humanity and personhood when fear occludes a clear view.

---

9. Connerton, *The Spirit of Mourning*, 33–50.

I do remember arriving in the room, though. This is imprinted on my brain like a videotape. It runs for just a few seconds before reverting to black, but those few seconds are precious.

We knocked to let Philip and Matthew know we had arrived. Kathleen went in first, opening the door to her new home. The sun was streaming in the two adjacent windows like a cliché of an English summer, and light filled the room. Kathleen walked to the middle and stood next to the yellow wing chair. She looked around her and clapped her hands.

'This is wonderful,' she enthused, genuine delight filling her features. 'And look, my things. How have you done all this? You are both so very clever.'

She looked at her nephews in turn, wonderment in her eyes. That they could have recreated her home in a brand new place was a miracle for her. She placed a proprietorial hand on the back of the armchair, and it was as if she had never been more at home anywhere else. In many ways, this furniture suited her better than the sagging Ercol suite that had been left behind in the bungalow.

In my mind's eye, the sun is dancing in the room. Philip and Matthew recede in my memory and I see Kathleen centre stage, owning her garret. The piano was neatly installed, and her clothes were arranged in the wardrobe. Her thimble collection was displayed on the shelf together with her cranberry glass and figurine. In the en-suite bathroom, her hairspray, Astral, hand-cream and Imperial Leather were lined up in orderly fashion. Her lipstick and face powder were on the ledge next to her comb and a mirror. There were no pill boxes and no notes. Kathleen was at home. The daily paper was artfully placed to disguise the functional, care home table that was designed so that it could be swung across a bed or an armchair.

Future copies of *The Times* would be delivered to this room, her meals would be prepared and someone else would take over her medical care. I would still take her to the dentist and optician but quickly learnt the need to forewarn Bluebell House so that they could furnish me with a list of current medication that I was no longer party to.

We were handing her over into someone else's care.

I think, in some ways, this adjustment was harder for me. My brain harboured regrets which Alzheimer's made impossible for Kathleen. The disease is a friend in this way. I had become used to being Kathleen's right-hand woman. I was an essential component on the team that was working together to negotiate life with Alzheimer's. Residential care would reduce me to just a visitor who signed-in, rather than a friend with my own key. The staff were strangers and I didn't yet trust them to look after my friend as well as I had done up to now.

What hubris. What selfishness. I didn't realise then that the moment of arrival hailed the beginning of the end of Kathleen's anxieties over money, over cleaning, shopping and the running of daily life. If I had been more honest, I would have reminded myself that Kathleen sometimes appeared at the door of her bungalow with hair uncombed and tears in her eyes, baffled and anxious at her own confusion. I would have acknowledged that she was often emotional and overwrought when I arrived, and that she needed me to re-centre her, rescue her from the fog. At Bluebell House, she need never get to that stage. There were plenty of Karens to reassure her.

But I couldn't stop thinking that this was the woman who had left home to attend university in 1946, was made Head of Geography in her first post, bought two houses, one direct from a new-build plan, welcomed her sick mother into her home, popping back every lunchtime from her job as deputy head to check she was alright, been a church warden, an education officer and a trustee of a charity. This was a woman who had travelled the world on her own and put significant money aside for just such an eventuality as this. This was a woman who had proved her capacities, her capabilities, her integrity and her intelligence time and time again. Wouldn't being in a care home immediately render her less?

I hadn't anticipated that Bluebell House would become the place where Kathleen could finally lay down life's responsibilities and enjoy the rest.

Kathleen did not cry when she left her home. All her weeping had been for the time before when the shock of diagnosis was raw. But returning to her bungalow on the evening of her departure floored me. I didn't need to go back then, but something compelled me to do it. I trailed around each room, wanting to feel her absence, to test the emptiness. I had nothing to do. With Kathleen gone, the only useful task was to water the hanging baskets, blooming in spite of everything. I closed her curtains so it would look like she was still there. That first night, it was me who pulled her door closed, checking I had the key. As I walked down her drive, I was swamped by the lack of my friend and I wept for what had been lost.

I know now that it was grief I was feeling. No one had died, but to me it felt comparable. She was gone from the place she had previously occupied and it was as if the fibres of the carpet cried out for her. As I watered the plants and turned her key in the lock, I didn't care who saw me cry. I didn't care if the neighbours' curtains twitched as I sobbed my way up Kathleen's drive that was no longer hers and walked the familiar path back to my house.

11
In the Margins

We had been advised to let Kathleen settle, to give her time to become familiarised with the routines of Bluebell House. For Philip and Matthew, this was easy. Reassured by Kathleen's delight at her new room, they could face the journeys back to Devon and Nottinghamshire with lighter hearts. Their aunt was safe and she had made the best start she could have done. For me, it was less straightforward. I took the gently given advice to mean stay away for a while, don't visit too often at first. I may have been oversensitive to kindly words meant to give confidence to Philip and Matthew, but I fought to keep feelings of rejection at bay.

Looking back, it was probably an unusual situation. The Bluebell House team had Philip as the first number to call in an emergency; he was the one who would be paying their bills and liaising over any additional medication and expenditure. Philip was family and I was a random other who happened to be close to one of their new residents. In all the years Kathleen lived there, I don't recall any other non-family member who was a primary visitor.

Sensitive to the needs of his aunt, and responding to a growing trust and affection between us, Philip took time to take the matron to one side and explain that Kathleen and I were good friends and that I had been caring for his aunt throughout the ups and downs of dementia so far. Should Kathleen be taken ill or be upset, they should call me. It was agreed that I would be the local point of contact, but I also made it clear that I did not expect to be included in any decisions over Kathleen's care.

Once I had waved off the boys, watered the plants and drawn the curtains in the bungalow I felt a loss I had not anticipated. Kathleen had made me realise how important it is to our wellbeing to be useful, and now I felt that I had handed over my usefulness to someone else. The only responsibility I had left was to oversee the periphery – pop to the local hospital to collect hearing aid batteries, make sure she had dental and optical appointments … it was a speck compared to what I had been doing, and it felt like demotion.

I consoled myself that there was unfinished business at the bungalow. If seeing Kathleen daily was not in her best interest, and if I'm honest it probably wasn't in mine, then I needed to fill the gaps with Kathleen-related activity until we got used to the routine. Who was I kidding? It was me who needed to get used to it. Kathleen had Alzheimer's; I knew her concept of time was skewed. She would have no idea whether I visited each day or each week. She was absolutely fine.

The bungalow would need to be sold, but Philip wasn't putting it on the market until he was certain that Kathleen was settled. In the meantime, those books were still sitting snugly in their shelves, begging to be sorted.

I filled my afternoons knee-deep in titles that had been collected over the previous fifty years, relishing the insights they gave me to Kathleen's former life. *The Forsyte Saga* in Penguin orange volumes was complete and well-thumbed. The print was excruciatingly small and I knew it was no longer possible for Kathleen to tolerate the font. They went into a box to go to my house; a little bit of Kathleen to add to my library. Philip and Matthew had taken all they wanted when they had been here for the move. I had their blessing to sort the rest.

Lots went to charity shops, some I reserved for the shelf by her bed at Bluebell House, others I saved so that I could rotate the titles, working in the same way as Kathleen's supplementary wardrobe in my loft. The ambition of this proposal was not evident until I had the benefit of hindsight. In the five years she was in the care home, she looked at only two books – dementia had stolen her capacity to follow a narrative, the opening hook lost before any development or climax could take place. Novels became little more than words without context. Neither of us had accepted this as fact at the time of her move. We were both equally enthusiastic about me storing additional volumes in my attic. For Kathleen, this was a holding on of selfhood – she was a person who read – for me, looking back, it was more evidence that I was wilfully blind to some of the detriments already wrought by Alzheimer's. Her library had become little more than a museum of something she used to do.

Kathleen never stopped identifying herself as a reader, noting down titles of books that Terence recommended in his weekly phone calls to his sister. Sometimes, seeing the scribbled messages she had written, she would ask me to buy a certain title. I did at first, but they were never read; the bookmark never moving beyond the opening pages, so I learnt to talk about Terence's enthusiasm whilst removing the note by sleight of hand. Kathleen hated unnecessary spending. If we were out shopping and I happened upon a skirt or a jumper that took my fancy, her resonant tones would sound from behind me:

'Walk on, Karen, walk on,' and she steered me by the elbow away from temptation.

Kathleen did not approve of excess. She would not want me to buy books that she would never read.

She also hated waste, so I was determined that what was left in her bungalow would be re-homed. Philip had given lots of kitchen equipment to a young family member who was heading out to live independently for the first time. His daughters and nieces had mementos of Aunty Kathleen's home, a place they remembered fondly from their own childhoods. Philip sorted the furniture. The books were my job.

One category of titles I thought it would be simple to rehouse were the Christian books. Accumulated over decades these covered apologetics, meditations, biographies, commentaries, Bibles and essays. She even had a novelisation of Jesus' life from the point of view of the disciples. Our church has a lending library and my first thought was to box everything up and drive them over. But something stopped me. Rather like diaries, religious books can reveal perhaps more than we'd want to share with others. Kathleen was a note-maker and I wanted to be sure that I wasn't donating more than books to the wider congregation.

We can find out a lot about people from the margins of their lives. Our public face often belies the eddies and currents that flow beneath the surface. And so it was here. In sorting her books, I got to know my friend at a deeper level, reading in the margins things she would never have uttered out loud. I read of her worries and concerns, of her prayers, doubts and delights.

These annotated texts never went to the church library. I boxed them up to go to Bluebell House; they were private reflections and needed to stay with Kathleen. But there were too many for the tiny bookshelf in her room and I worried that strangers might read her words. In the end I recycled the practical and erudite study notes but kept the two or three texts that had spilled Kathleen's heart to me.

I realised that through these notes to self, I had read of a Kathleen that no one had ever had access to. It was a Kathleen who mourned her single status and hoped for a husband even as late as her retirement. She wrote of trying to keep confidence in God's plans for her which had been different from her own wishes. In moments of trust, we had spoken of the fact that she had never had a romantic relationship. I knew that she had considered herself, bespectacled and ginger, as less attractive than her peers. I knew that she had never expected anyone to fall in love with her. But I hadn't known of her longing for a husband until I read pencilled prayers down the sides of the print where she fought to accept that busyness and service to others was to be her marriage.

She wrote of anguish over losses in the family, of untimely deaths and marriages breaking down. She wrote of loneliness and she wrote of thankfulness. She wrote her heart.

These books I took with me to Bluebell House and, tucked behind her other tomes, I was certain I had found a place where staff and other visitors would not easily find them. A deep recess in the wall served as a bookcase and the titles on the front were the ones that gathered dust for the next half-decade. These included *Purple Hibiscus,* a biography of John Stott, several blue, green and red leatherbound books, testifying to a time before the advent of the book jacket, and declaring the young Kathleen as a diligent student in their inked, handwritten bookplates and a Bible that had been presented at her confirmation – all were testimony to a past that told Kathleen's story as effectively as a photograph. All now collecting new motes of Bluebell House dust to settle on a lifetime. Behind these were nestled the books that told even deeper truths.

They stayed there, quickly forgotten by Kathleen and by me. Once the sorting had been done, her old life was dismantled, and new routines replaced those we had been used to. Kathleen's brain never computed the enormous change – she accepted her new life very easily and that made it simpler for me to do the same. I didn't think of the books again until weeks after her death when I received a phone call from Philip. He had been sorting the boxes we had hurriedly thrown together when we needed to clear her room at Bluebell House.

'Did you know about the notes in Kathleen's books?' he asked.

Though I hadn't thought of them at all since I had placed them in the recess, not even when we were sorting her room and contemplating the end of her life, I knew immediately what he meant.

'Ah,' I said. 'Yes. I'm really sorry I didn't think to warn you.'

'I never knew. I never knew she had been so lonely. She never told us. We could never have guessed.' His voice cracked.

'She didn't want you to know,' I said gently. 'She would never have wanted you to know.'

It was this certainty that made me hide the books in the first place, that stopped me from sharing what I had read. There were many margins full of earnest pencil prayers. I never read them all. Just enough to know that they were private, that they were meant for no one but Kathleen and God. Too precious to be thrown away, I had archived them and forgotten them. The little I did read made me love her more. Philip now feels the same.

12
A New Rhythm

Family relations, especially when lived at a distance, become subject to nostalgia and dependent on snapshots. Whilst Philip and Matthew shared history with Kathleen that spanned their whole lives, I knew the older version of their aunt perhaps even better than they did. I certainly felt, as she moved to Bluebell House, that I had the best knowledge of her Alzheimer's, how she reacted to things, how to negotiate and manage the disease so that she could live the best life that she could.

As I write this, I am amazed by my confidence. It didn't feel arrogant at the time; it felt like I was protecting Kathleen, shielding her from the judgement of others, enabling her to stay connected with who she had been. But I had no expertise in dementia; I had no real knowledge of the disease that was quietly shutting down connections in Kathleen's limbic system. I was handing her over to the care of those who knew more than I did about Alzheimer's, but they didn't know more than I did about Kathleen. The move to Bluebell House meant a new rhythm for both of us.

Amazingly, once Kathleen moved in, it seemed as though she had always been there. She was at home. For me, it was only after the transition that I fully understood how much it was needed. The snapshots of Kathleen's life afforded by occasional visits and the separation of over a hundred miles meant that Philip more clearly saw and readily accepted what I had found so difficult to admit.

Knowledge and love accrued over a lifetime served him better than my zealous protection of her later years.

The change in Kathleen was immediate and astonishing. Where I had anticipated confusion, there was contentment, and where I had expected anxiety, there was its absolute opposite. Daily life had become too much for Kathleen on her own. The fact that I popped in each day was very little in comparison with the hours she had to manage on her own. This was something I hadn't properly considered, and something which being in Bluebell House totally mitigated.

Being pragmatic and considering myself relatively empathetic, I navigated Kathleen's Alzheimer's as I went along. I was never the mother who read lots of childcare books, preferring to feel my way by intuition and common sense, and it was only after Kathleen had died that I read extensive accounts of living with dementia and its effect on the neurological and emotional landscape. Perhaps my reading was a form of grief, a consolidation of the previous decade. This whole book is somewhat of a catharsis, a reflection of what we learnt together and how we grew to understand each other more through our shared experience of navigating her life with dementia.

Alzheimer's disease alters the emotional landscape and living with it can be likened to the sensory overload we commonly associate with autistic spectrum disorder.[1] This I understood, having taught many students on the spectrum. Clearing the noise and clutter of classroom life to enable a student to learn was something I had tried to adapt to, though I hadn't made the connection with Alzheimer's. The hippocampus is our central tank for episodic memory and the amygdala is the control hub for emotional response. Both are situated beneath the medial-temporal lobe in the limbic system of the brain. In neurological scans of those with dementia and autism, these areas are shown to be the most compromised, making it harder for people living with these conditions to process external stimulus.[2] Thus the everyday sounds of conversation, doorbells, telephones, television, radio and even the more mundane humming of a fridge

---

1. 'A Sensory Lens to Explain Sundowning.' *Sensory Modulation Brisbane* (blog), January 14, 2022, http://sensory-modulation-brisbane.com/sensory-modulation-blog/a-sensory-lens-to-explain-sundowning#:~:text=This%20could%20apply%20to%20people,feelings%20of%20distress%20and%20overwhelm.

2. Poulin et al., 'Amygdala Atrophy Is Prominent in Early Alzheimer's Disease and Relates to Symptom Severity.'

or flushing of a toilet can become overwhelming. When considered alongside changing taste buds and damage to olfactory processing, it is easy to see that living with dementia is a constant process of trying to exist in a world that is becoming increasingly overwhelming.[3]

Shrinking Kathleen's world to a bed-sitting room with an en-suite wet room was therefore not a reduction for her, but a simplification. It was too easy for me to continue to measure the quality of her life against what she had always known. The move to Bluebell House was a challenge for me to think differently. Where I might rail against reduction in circumstance or removal of autonomy, for Kathleen, it was relief. I lacked the imagination to understand any of that until I saw the almost instant improvement in her wellbeing once she had moved.

Prior to the move, I made sure that we chatted about her new house, her room and the gardens, trying to ensure that she had some form of context for the upheaval. Prompted by activities at home, she pondered her new life.

'Will I be able to make you a cup of tea when you come?'

From our visit, I knew there was a communal kitchen on the lower floor. We had needed to go down two flights of stairs to get to it. It was so small that only one person could squeeze into the tight gap between the wall and the counter. I didn't think it would be a space residents would be encouraged to use. Practising hospitality was perhaps something Kathleen would have to give up.

I soon found out, however, that it was practised by Bluebell House on their behalf. Visitors were welcomed and tea and biscuits procured if desired; and once Kathleen settled in, it was as though she had always enjoyed her own set of kitchen staff to serve her visitors and make her meals. She didn't mourn the lack of autonomy because the absence of responsibility enabled her to relax.

'It's like being in a hotel,' she explained, beaming. 'I go down for breakfast and then its elevenses and then lunch.'

The security of an institution cannot be underestimated, and I think that for a teacher like Kathleen, there was another level of comfort to be gained from the rhythm of the Bluebell House day. I quickly learnt that if I wanted to take Kathleen out for coffee, I needed to arrive by 10 a.m. She had written notes to remind her of the times of breakfast, coffee, lunch, tea and dinner – these were

---

3. 'Houston_a_report_2016_final.Pdf.'

displayed prominently on her chest of drawers. She copied out a small version for her handbag and, if she was ever concerned that I might be keeping her out too long, she would begin to root around in there to check the piece of card. Bath morning was Friday and after a couple of false starts when I bowled up for a visit, I was gently reminded by the nursing staff that if I could help them maintain their routine, it would be better for Kathleen.

The bathroom was a very sumptuous affair too. I was not going to come between Kathleen and this weekly luxury. Adapted so that residents with all manner of difficulties could access the bath, it was more like a spa or therapy pool than a facility for a wash. Equipped with jets and bubbles, this became a highlight of the week and an 'appointment' that Kathleen wrote in her diary.

I still felt slightly disenfranchised; I had handed over Kathleen's care to people I didn't know. Trust takes time and I wasn't there yet. A big part of me missed the intimacy of visiting Kathleen at the bungalow, of negotiating diaries and supervising her food consumption. I am a practical person, more able to show affection through a clean house and a cooked meal than through the fripperies of romance. I was now unable to show my love for Kathleen through what I did. In essence, there was nothing for me to actually do. Bluebell House was now responsible for all medical supervision. She no longer needed me to shop for her – Bluebell House provided all food and drink. She no longer needed me to be vigilant over her diet – she was now regularly weighed, and food and nutrition adapted according to her changing needs. Philip still sent me an allowance to use for clothing and toiletries, but I felt like a spare part where I had once been essential.

This is where I gleaned the most important lesson of all. Though Kathleen had needed me to help her negotiate an increasingly noisy and unfamiliar world, she now just needed a friend. I thought back to the years prior to dementia when we had chatted in the car, when she had offered me salient advice. I knew Kathleen well and she knew me. What better basis for continuing a friendship? For her remaining years, I could stop being her carer, stop looking out for signs of further decline, and instead just enjoy her company.

It was easier to do this in Bluebell House. The last things we surrender are the essential parts of what makes us who we are. Even in advanced dementia, when procedural memory fails and people become totally dependent on others, awareness of being loved is retained. When speech has gone, we still respond to a warm voice or gentle touch – the stroke of a cheek, the squeeze of a hand.[4] Kathleen was only in the moderate stages of Alzheimer's disease when she arrived at Bluebell House; indeed, the relief she experienced in surrendering the cooking, cleaning, washing and accounting was such that she seemed to bounce back a few years. Dementia seemed less significant there because her life had been simplified. Overload had been rectified and she was ready to live differently.

Kathleen's transition to a care facility was very successful. This isn't always the case for people living with Alzheimer's, and I think the key for Kathleen was that she moved before her dementia became disabling. She had never been found wandering and lost; she had continued walking to the local shop each day. Although I helped her with household tasks, generally it was still Kathleen who pushed the vacuum cleaner around or washed up the tea things. She was muddled and vulnerable but was still reasonably independent.

Commenting on Kathleen's positive start at Bluebell House, the matron told me that this wasn't the case for all new admissions. She told me that although it is possible to thrive in a nursing home environment, there seems to be a pattern. People either settle and stay for years or they see their arrival as some sort of defeat and give up.

No longer required to deal with Kathleen's everyday needs I began to enjoy the freedom of being her friend. Resident at Bluebell House for over five years, it was only in the latter months that Kathleen was confined to barracks. Until then, I saw my role as an enabler, someone who could take Kathleen out and ensure her horizons were not constrained to the perimeter of the care home. We would often be found in various Berkshire cafés and garden centres, joking that we could write a guide to all the local tearooms. If the weather was cold, we'd sometimes go for a tree-lined drive and admire the winter branches decorated in the white of an early frost. Sometimes we'd bundle up for an adventure, defying the Bluebell House timetable.

'I've booked you out for lunch today.'

'Have you signed us out in the book?'

'I have indeed.'

---

4. Taylor, *The Fragile Brain*, .

The rhythms of the care home, should, cognitively, have been harder for Kathleen to grasp than they were – dementia always shows impairment in the ability to compute new learning – but Kathleen absorbed the times and expectations of Bluebell House logistics far more quickly than I thought possible.[5] Years of constructing timetables and imposing conformity on others at work had presumably programmed her to accept such routine as a sensible matter of course. She relied on the notes around her bedroom and down the margin of her diary that indicated Bluebell House timings, but she soon learnt the rhythm of the days and, perhaps more significantly, learnt to surrender her routine to the staff. If Kathleen failed to come down for a meal, someone would be sure to notice and follow up with a knock on her door, and a friendly care worker then accompanied her down the grand flight of stairs for dinner.

It didn't take long for Kathleen to become a champion of her new home.

'This is where I live now and I'm jolly lucky to be here. The staff are all so kind. Anyone who complains ... well, if anyone complained, then I should like to have a few words with them!'

This willingness to submit positively is testimony to Kathleen, and a quality she demonstrated throughout her life. Her father died when she was still a young woman – his death sudden and unexpected. This profoundly affected her, and she spoke with disbelief whenever she revisited that time. It made her proactive in taking exercise. Like me, she was more comfortable in action than emotion. From his passing, Kathleen ensured that she walked daily. Heart failure was not going to be her swansong if she could prevent it. Unwittingly, she was also providing armour against Alzheimer's, as exercise and the subsequent oxygenation of the brain is thought to be beneficial in maintaining cerebral health.[6]

With his death, Kathleen realised that her mother, who had been battling aplastic anaemia for some years, would not be able to manage on her own. Recognising that her brother had his own family commitments, Kathleen discounted the responsibilities she now held as a deputy head teacher and brought her mother to live with her.

---

5. Nilsson and Ohta, *Dementia and Memory*, 157.

6. Radak et al., 'Exercise Plays a Preventative Role in Alzheimer's Disease,' 777.

'It was the only thing to do. I couldn't leave her in Surrey on her own.'

'Wasn't that very hard for you to manage?'

'Not really. Not at first, anyway. Mummy wasn't unwell all the time, so in the beginning it was lovely to come home from work and have my dinner cooked for me.'

'What about later on?'

'That was harder,' she conceded. 'I lived near school, so I would go home every lunch hour to check on Mum and make sure she had something to eat. Going out in the evenings was impossible and I made sure all hospital appointments coincided with school holidays. I attended multiple blood transfusions with her. It was hard. But I'm glad I did it.'

Kathleen approached the move to Bluebell House as just another example of a life change which she would face with gratitude. Looking back, it is this quality that permeated her friendship with me. She was always thankful for every little thing I did, and she was remarkably easy to please.

'I've had a lovely morning, dear. Thank you.'

'Nice of you to say so, but we've only been to the chemists.'

'It's just lovely to be out.'

We could all learn a lot from such simplicity. Dementia forces those living with it to have a sharper focus on the present. The recent past is lost and the future hard to visualise, so the moment becomes more precious. Ironically, it is mindfulness in practice. Kathleen may not have remembered we had only been to the chemists or the supermarket, but she responded to the company, to the feelings she experienced when we were together. Every day could thus be a lovely day.

As the dementia progressed, Kathleen learnt to surrender more responsibility to others. She learnt that there was a freedom in depending on other people. When we were out, she was confident that I would ensure she had all she needed. She called me her PA and Philip her financial advisor – I would remember for her and keep her diary and Philip would run the finances. This spin on amnesia was a very positive way to approach decreasing mental cognition. It was also some proof that, though she couldn't remember our days out or whether Philip had visited, she retained the core of who she was. We may have become her guides to navigate a life impeded by

Alzheimer's, but her soul remained as positive, sensible and humble as it always had been.

Despite such a positive start to residential care, I was warned by the House Manager that it might not take long for Kathleen to become institutionalised, that she might become reluctant to leave the safe confines of the home. And she was right. The security of a timetable and organised activities meant that, in many ways, leaving Bluebell House was unnecessary.

It was quickly apparent that, though not necessary, regular sojourns away from the house were enormously beneficial. If I had been on holiday and Kathleen hadn't been out for a couple of weeks, then her Alzheimer's symptoms were more pronounced. She was more confused and increasingly anxious. I then had to conquer her anxiety by persuading her to come out with me, reassuring her that if she was with me then she would be fine, that if she felt uneasy at any point then I would bring her straight back. The positive effects of memory loss also came into play here – I knew that once I had got her out of the front door, then she would forget her worry about leaving it. She would exclaim about the weather, express delight that my car had coincidentally got her initials in the number plate and then we would be off.

I had thought my job was just to be Kathleen's friend, but it was more important than that – I was guardian of her world view. If she was to resist institutionalisation, then I needed to take her out of Bluebell House. She was no longer able to book a plane ticket to Australia or a coach trip to Alnwick, but together we ensured that she saw more of life than was afforded by the slow pace and patterns of residential life.

13
Christmas Selves

Following her diagnosis, I saw Kathleen become increasingly insecure in recollecting yesterday or last week, but correspondingly more confident in sharing tales of her remote past. This pattern continued throughout the course of the disease until she spent more time recalling snapshots from her childhood than she did engaging with the present. Scientists explain this by the fact that even with sustained damage to the hippocampus, patients with dementia often present with a temporal gradient to their retrograde amnesia – in other words, memories from further back remain clear whilst more recent experiences are inaccessible.[1]

Kathleen's grasp on the present was limited to a few minutes; living with Alzheimer's had almost wiped her short-term memory, making her dependent on the tiny window of working memory for everyday conversation. Discussion of the future was uncertain for a different reason. Forward-planning is often compromised in those living with Alzheimer's disease, another complication of atrophy in the hippocampal region. Contemplation of what might lie ahead lacks context, resulting in fear and anxiety.[2]

It is believed that older memories are more consolidated than recent ones; they are less dependent on the hippocampal region

---

1. Ólafsdóttir, Bush and Barry, 'The Role of Hippocampal Replay in Memory and Planning,' 37.

2. Mitchell, *Somebody I Used to Know*, 80.

and rely more on the central cortex of the brain.[3] Kathleen's youth had been sufficiently rehearsed and therefore could be more readily retold. Remote memories are encoded in their appropriate brain areas – so visual recollections are stored in the visual cortex whilst emotional responses to a past event will be collected in the amygdala. These groups of neurons are ready to be fired up as a single unit to reproduce a specific memory.[4] With information stored in multiple places, long-term memories are more resilient to the dementing process than new memories.

Such resilience was evident in conversation with Kathleen. She entertained me with stories that she remembered fondly and enjoyed retelling. As a child she lived in a cul-de-sac in Redhill. Now a Surrey commuter town with an ever-widening perimeter, the way she described it depicts a quiet, country existence. Her father was a policeman and her mother a housewife – he wouldn't countenance the thought of a wife who worked. They had a garden where he grew vegetables. There were roses in the summer and dahlias in the autumn. During her school days, Kathleen would cut off the corner of a long walk by taking a shortcut through the garden and over the back fence before scooting up the hill for a bus to Reigate Grammar School for Girls.

Kathleen remembered a childhood of Sunday dinners with her grandad, cooked and served by Mrs Rivers, the Methodist housekeeper who had lived-in since Grandad's widowhood. Her Methodism meant she didn't attend the same church as the Barr family whilst her propriety ensured that she only ever ate with them on Christmas Day. Kathleen tells me that these Sunday dinners were a special privilege afforded only to her. There was only ever her and Grandad at the table over roast beef and Yorkshire pudding with a generous helping of Mrs Rivers' gravy. She assumed that her brother and her parents ate at home but could not fathom an explanation for this.

'It seems strange now that you ask. I have no idea why; it was just how it was.'

Since these conversations, I have learnt from Terence that these sumptuous lunches were not only for Kathleen. He remembers that

---

3. Ólafsdóttir, Bush, and Barry, 'The Role of Hippocampal Replay in Memory and Planning,' 37.

4. The Human Memory, 'Memory Storage – Memory Processes.'

they alternated Sundays; their parents convinced that whilst each child could be depended upon to behave individually, if allowed to visit together, too much mischief would ensue! Kathleen had been able to access her own memory, but not the detail that went with it.

It was at her grandfather's house that she learnt the piano. Whilst he snoozed after lunch, she would take herself to the drawing room and carefully lift the lid. She would sit, back straight, patiently picking out notes, later daring to try tunes and chords.

'And he never once woke up,' she chuckled. 'I had to prove to my parents that I was serious about my music. I had to show them that I'd managed to learn something on my own before they were prepared to pay for my lessons.'

When she was ten, she was deemed to have served her apprenticeship and she was rewarded with regular tuition.

The piano was a comfort to Kathleen throughout the experience of early and moderate stages of Alzheimer's disease. Procedural musical memory can be spared in those living with dementia, suggesting that there may be a specialised memory system for music that is distinct from other domains such as verbal and visual memory.[5] Terence, Kathleen's younger brother, implicitly recognised the importance of music in his sister's life and he saw it as key to her retaining an essential part of who she had always been. Seeing her decreasing confidence post-diagnosis, he wanted to make certain that the piano was accessible to her for as long as possible. He persuaded Kathleen into our local piano shop to spend some of her hard-earned savings, not on more sheet music, but on a brand-new instrument, one that had sockets for headphones and a volume control. His foresight meant that she was able to transport this new piano with her to Bluebell House – a key factor in enabling Kathleen to preserve her sense of self once she had entered residential care.

The new piano gave Kathleen renewed enthusiasm for life, gave her something to think about beyond the confusion and fear that often enveloped her without warning. She organised the removal of her old instrument to a new home across the road where there lived a little girl eager to start lessons.

'It's so good to be able to help someone else start out,' Kathleen smiled as she waved the old piano off the premises, 'I hope she enjoys it as much as I have done.'

---

5. Baird and Samson, 'Memory for Music in Alzheimer's Disease,' 85.

117

The new instrument was set up in her bungalow in the spot vacated by the acoustic piano. Terence explained the volume control and set it all up, and she was away, delighted in the decadence of her new purchase.

I don't think she ever changed the settings – it was already too late to teach Kathleen new technology – as far as she was concerned, pianos were as loud as the pressure that was exerted on the key. Beethoven, Debussy, Bach, Chopin and Mozart regularly tripped off her ageing fingertips. Kathleen was convinced that a lifetime at the piano had kept arthritis at bay, that it had sustained her in difficult times and allowed her space to relax in the midst of competing demands. When we were out, she would often flex her hands, spanning her fingers to form a chord or span an octave.

'Are your hands stiff?'

'No, just stretching them, keeping them supple. Sometimes they get a little cold.'

I remember this action fondly. We miss the little things that make up a person when they are gone. I remember Kathleen if ever I stretch my own ageing hands in the car, encouraging circulation in the cold. She is present in much of what I do.

We spoke of the wonder of muscle memory, Kathleen voicing amazement that she could forget something as simple as what she had done ten minutes ago, and yet her hands remembered their way around a keyboard. As Terence had wisely predicted, playing the instrument gave her solace, a balm to the confusion that threatened her independence and invaded her perception of herself. It was with affection that we noticed he had added his own handwriting to the increasing number of notes around her bungalow. It simply read *Play the piano every day.*

Music has been a common thread of positivity in the experience of many of those living with Alzheimer's. My mum's best friend, even in the most advanced stage of dementia when all procedural functions had been compromised, could occasionally mouth the words of a cherished hymn. Kathleen, in the Christmas before she died, could join in a carol with a descant learnt in her youth, reaching the high notes easier than me. My colleague Lisa, whose father had frontal temporal lobe dementia, also testified to the relief that music brought to her dad.

'Songs still had connections for him. He used to be a DJ, so I played lots of upbeat, 80s tracks in the car. He danced to the rhythm and made noises that were his efforts at words. If he stopped jigging about, I changed the track.[6]

Power of faith and song and art are now recognised as elements which are resistant to the ravages of dementia. Watching such connection with lyrics or music or poetry or painting has been described 'like a flower reviving in water,' leading to the conclusion that 'people with Alzheimer's need to be drenched in art.'[7] Watching her father join in with lyrics during a family singsong, where previously his 'tangled-up, snarled-up, muddled-up mind' seemed to have lost its way in almost everything, Nicci Gerrard writes of the painful delight in seeing evidence of 'words he had loved long ago still delicately chime.' Moments such as these can occur even in the most advanced stages of dementia. They are echoes of a voice that speak to us of character and personality that is not entirely lost, a voice in the darkness that 'speaks *I am here, I am here, I was always here.*'[8]

The pathology of Alzheimer's disease initially affects the temporal lobes, an area of the brain important in retrieving semantic and episodic memories. The expectation from a neurological perspective then is that a person living with dementia should experience impairment in retrieval of long-term musical memory. The fact that it does not, that the brain regions mediating musical memory seem to be spared by Alzheimer's pathology until its very late stages, is difficult to fathom.[9] It is as if music enters the core of selfhood, and, like the emotional self, is hard to eradicate.

Kathleen's first Christmas at Bluebell House marked five months as a resident. Prompted by shortening days and cards beginning to arrive with the morning post, Kathleen retold the story of previous cold December mornings when she would get up for her festive holiday job at the local post office. She had to start early, and, muffled against the winter, walked briskly down the steep hill, where she would frequently meet her father on his way up, returning from a night shift at the local police station. He would have abandoned the attempt to ride his bicycle and, instead, be pushing it alongside

---

6. LS interview.

7. Gerrard, *What Dementia Teaches Us about Love*, 148.

8. Gerrard, 144.

9. Baird and Samson, 'Memory for Music in Alzheimer's Disease,' 89.

him. Weary, but still immaculate in his uniform and bobby's helmet, Kathleen remembered them exchanging cheery greetings.

This simple memory, like so many, is fragmented. It is a vivid picture, but the film reel doesn't run for long. I was told of these wintry encounters on the hill many times, but never with more detail or context than that which I relate here. It is a moment retold, showing her affection for her father and continued amusement that he was coming home whilst she was going out.

Kathleen commonly accessed remote memories like this when prompted by something in the present. I first heard this one when we wrote her Christmas cards together back in her bungalow in the years when I was just giving her a hand, when we were both denying the possibility of Alzheimer's. Surrounding us was the carefully managed display of her own Season's Greetings. Kathleen's penchant for order really tickled my daughter when she was young. On the bookcase in her lounge and on the mantlepiece were cards depicting the nativity. The real meaning of Christmas always got centre stage. As your eyes followed the room, a tale would unfold: angel cards came first, followed by the shepherds, the manger and the three wise men. Acceptable, but would never be sent by Kathleen were the wintry depictions of robins and holly and ivy. Finally, subordinated to the very bottom shelves of the dining room bookcase were cards which showed Santa, reindeers and presents.

That first Christmas at Bluebell House, she persisted in this arrangement of her cards, but in subsequent years she forgot that she had ever had such a system. Instead, I Blu-Tacked them in rank order on her behalf, fighting a losing battle with cards put up by the staff who didn't know what had always been.

Still a competent pianist that first year, she was eager to set up a tradition of a carol service by the residents for the residents. She was to choose the songs, play them on her piano and lead the whole lounge in seasonal celebration. Years of organising school events and taking responsibility meant that Kathleen was confident she could achieve this goal. The matron agreed and we were both content that this was well within Kathleen's capabilities.

But, together with reduction in working memory, higher-order processing is particularly impeded by Alzheimer's in its middle stages, reducing the executive functions of creative and flexible thinking.[10] I was ignorant of this fact and, even had I known it, I think I would still have thought Kathleen perfectly suited to the task. She presented a calm and capable public self, and her conversations, though circular, remained erudite and articulate. She was adamant in her intent, and I was happy to believe she could do it. Looking back, it is easy to see that this was one of those occasions when I overestimated her functional ability. Such mismatch is common – both those with dementia and their primary caregivers consistently make such overestimations in the earlier and middle stages of the disease.[11] In wanting to preserve Kathleen's self-perception, I colluded. Of course she could put together nine lessons and carols, of course she could. Neither of us wanted to give Alzheimer's the upper hand.

Kathleen's responsibility for the running order of the carol service was quickly evidenced by an alarming number of notes perpetuating around her room. She had the order of service written out on a pad by her bedside table, another on the lap tray and more tucked into copies of *The Times* and on her dresser. When I visited, she looked exhausted, worn out by the task she had given herself. She began to look like she had done in the last weeks at the bungalow. Thinking of nothing else, her mind was on a loop and she could see nothing beyond the logistics and responsibility.

'I am so worried about this. I haven't decided on the carols. Do you think "Once In Royal" should be first?'

I gave her a hug, hoping that physical comfort might still her troubled mind. I reassured her that she had sorted it all out, that the songs had been decided and that the staff were really grateful to her.

Kathleen's anxiety took me back to the time before. Surely culling notes had belonged to earlier times of confusion? Once again, I found myself secreting paper, squirrelling multiple copies of the order of service into my bag, leaving her with just one set. I wrote a note in her diary – *Karen will type up the carol service so that I don't need to worry about it.*

Bringing it with me the following day, I had stapled a large-print message on the front page which read: *The carol service is sorted. I have done everything, and it is typed up here. The office has a copy of this. If I feel anxious, I can talk to a member of staff or ring Karen.*

---

10. Attix and Welsh-Bohmer, *Geriatric Neuropsychology*, 58.
11. Attix and Welsh-Bohmer, *Geriatric Neuropsychology*, 163.

I attended the carols. Practically, I was positioned as page-turner while Kathleen played the piano, but I was also her confidence, prompting her to the next part of the order of service, enabling her to lead her new friends in Christmas singing and praise. It went beautifully, but the effort exhausted her.

The document *Bluebell Carols* is still filed on my computer and a hard copy stored under *Kathleen* in my filing cabinet. She had wanted to create an annual event, but Alzheimer's was not going to let her do it again. Indeed, by the following year, only external activities and the date on her newspaper prompted her knowledge of it being Christmas.

External activities remained important, however, and a subsequent Christmas lunch at Bluebell House helped me to learn more about the persistence of self in advancing dementia. I was seated with Kathleen on a table with five residents and no other carers – I had clearly passed some sort of unspoken test with the management! Kathleen was in good form. She liked a formal occasion and was by this stage more confident in the care home environment than when out in the wider world. We sat and sipped aperitifs as I sussed out my companions for the afternoon.

Irene, on my left, was completely absorbed in her knife and fork, picking them up and putting them down in turn. 'These aren't mine,' she muttered repeatedly. Ernest, sitting opposite had a twinkle in his eye as he said hello. Kathleen, to my right, was most interested in the crackers. She may not have known it was Christmas before we came downstairs to the dining room, but the prompts of the table decorations and the crackers stirred understanding of context not yet undermined by Alzheimer's. Kathleen waved a cracker in the air and tried to whip up enthusiasm for them round the table.

'Let's pull our crackers then,' she said in a palimpsest of the jolly schoolteacher.

'What do we want to do that for?' grumbled Irene, looking up from her inspection of the cutlery.

'It's Christmas,' Kathleen insisted.

Her school-ma'am authority won the day and we took turns to pull them. They all wanted me to help. We read out jokes and exclaimed over the trinkets. Kathleen quickly slid her mini notebook into her handbag, not wanting to lose possession of her prize. Irene picked up her plastic comb and asked several times why she had it at the dinner table. In the meantime, she was hungry. Where was the food? Ernest laughed at everything.

I swear he grinned directly at me before pleating the tablecloth at his knees and beginning to tug it towards him.

'Ernest, that's the tablecloth,' I warned, reaching over to offer him the matching linen napkin instead.

His face broke into a broad smile as he lifted the edge of the cloth and shifted all our plates several centimetres towards his lap.

'Ernest!' I cried out, 'It's the tablecloth you're pulling!'

I attempted to tug the arrangement back in place and had the sense to snuff out the candle, just in case.

He grinned again and went to pull harder, lifting the excess length towards his chin.

'No!' I warned. 'Not the tablecloth.'

He laughed out loud then, dipped his head towards his lap and wiped his lips on the hem of the cloth. Then, with deliberation, he let it go and picked up the napkin as if nothing had happened. His eyes shone.

This was definitely a moment to remember that those living with dementia are still themselves. Ernest knew exactly what he was doing. In this way, dementia can be a playground. We whose faculties are as yet unimpaired can be very quick to denounce quirky behaviour as symptomatic of Alzheimer's but, more often than not, it is evidence for the resilience of self. Beneath confusion and loss of episodic memory, the strong strand of selfhood persists.

I learnt not to measure losses in the conventional way. Even though none of my companions would remember the meal or even that it was Christmas time, they each enjoyed the moment. There was pleasure in the food, in the crackers and in the mischief, and that pleasure was genuine. This remained the case for other aspects of life. Even when Kathleen had stopped playing piano, it continued to provide her with comfort and identity. The piano remained in position in the corner of her room, sheet music poised for animation. She was convinced that she played regularly, she loved it, would never miss a day – it helped to keep her relaxed in a busy life. It was something she could never give up.

Whilst we knew she had given up months, even years before her death, there was nothing to be gained by correcting her. Truth is sometimes a matter of perception, and it can be unwittingly cruel to insist on reality as a person without dementia sees it. Kathleen was a musician. Alzheimer's was not going to take that away from her – the loss we saw was not a loss she felt. She was a pianist. Holding onto that helped her to retain a sense of self until the very end. There is something fundamental about music that reaches beyond the fog.

14
Through a Glass Darkly

Photographs too, proved an excellent stimulus. An absolute benefit of moving into residential care meant that Philip had pared down Kathleen's massive collection to a few key boxes. He would switch them when he visited, ensuring variety and giving his aunt the opportunity to access different memories.

In the latter days, when she felt too weary to leave her wing chair and tour Berkshire's coffee shops with me, I would draw her attention to the old albums stacked in the corner of the room. Sometimes these photographs created a pathway for a memory that had been locked away, and I learnt something new about my friend. More often, they seemed to create a visual comfort blanket, an assurance that Kathleen had a past, even if she couldn't always access it.

Kathleen was adept at recognising her former self in old photographs. She smiled fondly at her youth and would retell key stories over and over. This wasn't the same when she looked in a mirror. As Alzheimer's progressed in its path through her brain, there seemed to be increasing mismatch between the image in the glass and the one she held of herself in her head.

'What's become of me? I'm such a sight.'

She would pull her pale green comb impatiently through her silvered hair and tut at her reflection.

'I don't know,' she sighed.

I thought little of this at the time, simply assuming that the ageing process causes most of us to regret the passing of time. Since then, I have learnt that mirrors can be a particular problem to a person living with Alzheimer's. Set up to make a room look bigger, they can distort spaces so that it is difficult to work out where reality ends and reflection begins. I hadn't considered this in my care of Kathleen; maybe she wasn't bothered by them, perhaps it was one of those things that she couldn't articulate, but it didn't seem like something she feared. It was obvious to my colleague Lisa that even early on in his dementia, her dad found mirrors appalling. She told me they had to remove all of them as her father was beginning to feel hunted, as though there were countless other people in the house. Even his own reflection was malevolent, a stranger who might mean harm.[1] Alongside the paranoiac distortion that mirrors can afford to some people with dementia, there is a more normalised emotional impact; a realisation that the person reflected back is not the face you remember or expect to see. The mirror tells its own story of the changes that Alzheimer's is making.[2] I think this is what Kathleen was seeing, and such revelation was startling every time she stood before the glass.

I also hadn't appreciated the link between visual deficit and dementia, finding it only in reading that I have done since Kathleen's death. It seems obvious now that the eyes are dependent on messages from the brain, using the very neuronal circuitry invaded by the plaques and tangles of Alzheimer's. Losing perception of depth makes tripping and falling increasingly likely as the visual cortex fails to decode messages that enable us to distinguish kerbs, changes in surfaces or thresholds.[3] I had assumed that Kathleen's increasingly tight grip on my arm as we walked to the car park, through town or along the river had been a result of age, a loss of physical confidence readily associated with the elderly. But perhaps it was another outworking of Alzheimer's.

Photographs are a much safer form of reflection, enabling someone living with dementia to make sense of themselves. Simultaneously, they can give access to a past proof of identity and capability whilst also providing a map for the future: 'when the

1. LS interview.
2. Mitchell, *Somebody I Used to Know*, 211.
3. VisionAware, 'How Alzheimer's Disease Affects Vision and Perception.'

memories have emptied on the inside, they'll be here on the outside – a constant, a reminder, a feeling of happier times.[4]

This was certainly the case with Kathleen. Photographs pictured her as she perceived herself, not as Alzheimer's had reformed her in the mirror. Clearing space in the scarf drawer at the care home some years after she had moved in, I found a brown envelope of loose pictures. In a faded white cardboard frame with the photographer's name and negative number written on the back was Kathleen's graduation photograph from 1949. She is twenty-two and standing tall with her mortar board at a jaunty angle. She wears small, round, dark spectacles and is smiling easily. Her hair defies gravity, rolled into a tall pleat at the back of her head, 'I can't remember how I did that,' she said as she traced her locks with a pearlescent pink fingernail.

This has become my favourite picture of Kathleen, more so than the many I have of her and me on various outings. Maybe it reminds me of who she was before I met her, if that is even possible, or maybe it makes me imagine the woman she was before age and Alzheimer's battled to make her less. I had it copied so that Kathleen now sits next to my grandparents in a silver frame on my bookcase.

It was not until 1920 that women were permitted to graduate in England, and so just two decades on from that, I regard Kathleen's success at gaining a place at Exeter University to study for an honours degree in Geography as pioneering. Exeter Schools of Art and Science were founded in 1851, elevated to University College of the South-West in 1922. On the website, its early history is all lumped together as *pre-1955*.[5] Firmly falling into that early category, Kathleen arrived at the railway station in September of 1946 with a single trunk.

She told several stories that persist from that time. On arrival at her digs, she felt very mature and sophisticated, but then confessed to being completely floored as she went to unpack and realised that the lock on her trunk was broken. Kathleen remembered standing with the trunk on the narrow bed and dealing it a few savage blows before crumpling on the candlewick bedspread in a fit of tears. Acutely aware that she was to be ten weeks away from home, she was

4.   Mitchell, *Somebody I Used to Know*, 17.

5.   University of Exeter, 'History | About Us.'

already missing the steadying reassurance and lock-picking skills of her father.

'That would not do,' she reported to me, as if chastising herself again for a moment of weakness. 'I realised that no one was going to help me, so I tried again.'

On that attempt, the lid popped open and her essential undergraduate wardrobe of long skirts and robes was freed from its tissue.

That was the only time she experienced homesickness, but, she recollected, the same could not be said of one of her roommates. There were three other girls in her first-year room and Kathleen was able to tell me that she was pretty sure one was Swedish, another was definitely called Janet and studied English (which, according to Kathleen, necessitated far less work than geography students were required to do) and then there was a nameless, 'hapless thing' who survived the ordeal of university life for less than a fortnight. This seared itself on Kathleen's memory as a period 'when the floods of Noah threatened to overpower our dorm. She started to cry as soon as she arrived, and the only respite we got from her weeping was when she finally gave in to sleep.'

Kathleen wasted no sentiment on the girl and confessed that she was very glad to arrive back from lectures one day and find the fourth bed stripped and all evidence of that particular roommate gone.

'It was as if she had just vanished, and, I'm ashamed to say now, I was really quite thankful for her departure.'

Photographs, and the memories they unlock, have been used as a therapy for those living with moderate and later stages of dementia. In the Netherlands, visual artist Laurence Aëgerter has developed a programme of images that are used to stimulate the imagination of those with Alzheimer's.[6] The photographs are not specific to their individual pasts, but are generic images, paired to encourage response and conversations. As short-term memory becomes less accessible, questions based on recall are likely to result in a sense of inadequacy or failure.[7] Such experiences can create feelings of isolation and contribute to those with dementia withdrawing into themselves. The purpose of photographic intervention is to stimulate

---

6. Photographic Treatment, 'About Us.'

7. CNN, 'A Photographic Treatment for Dementia'

memories or comment without pressure to remember any specific person or event.

Though Kathleen always enjoyed looking through her photographs, they did sometimes make her feel sad, exposing the difference between former self and current capacity. Looking at pictures of her post-retirement travels she commented,

'I can't believe I ever did all these things. I certainly couldn't do it now.'

And if she couldn't remember the people or the context of an image, she would be reminded of the reduction in her own capacity: 'I should know this, but I don't. It's like I'm looking at someone else's life.'

When this happened, I put the photos away, and, much like the intention behind the project in the Netherlands, I substituted personal photos for a much-loved pictorial geography of the world, where bright images of rainforests, waterfalls and volcanoes nudged at her academic interest and prompted educated comments that had been rehearsed in a lifetime of classrooms.

Another photograph from the envelope at the back of the drawer was a picture of three young women. They all have typical rolled, set hairstyles of the late 1940s, curling from their crowns to just below the shoulders. Kathleen is a head taller than the others. They wear summer dresses – cotton and full-skirted with hems to the top of the shin – and they are leaning against a giant haystack. On the back of the photo were names scribed in Kathleen's spidery writing. It is handwriting readily associated with old people, and yet this was produced with a strong hand, indenting the photographic paper quite deeply and made up of tiny, closely formed letters. These monikers were not a recent addition.

'Who are these, then?'

'Ah,' she paused.

Alzheimer's makes retrieval a slow and arduous process. I had made myself a rule that I wouldn't ask Kathleen anything if I had no scaffolding that could help her frame an answer. I didn't want to cause her any feelings of inadequacy or failure. But I had the names of the girls in the picture, so there was something I could offer if she needed a prompt.

'That's me,' she said confidently.

'And it says Marion and Sims on the back.' I gave her the information that she had kept in perpetuity with her biro notes.

129

'Well, that must have been one summer holiday. You've met Marion, haven't you?'

I had. She was Kathleen's sister-in-law.

'Sims?' I prompted.

'Yes – she was from South Africa and she came home with me in the university breaks sometimes.'

This was new information, a slice of Kathleen's life that hadn't bubbled to the surface before. The photograph had opened a pathway into her past. It was evident from her strong affirmation that Kathleen was certain about Sims.

'And the three of you were messing around in a farmer's hayfield?'

She chuckled, 'Oh yes. We used to do that every year!'

And that was that. Portal closed. Nothing more was forthcoming, no details and no embellishment. It was a fact she was certain of, could see captured on a photograph spotted with age, but with no additional biography. I never learnt anything more about Sims.

15
A Sense of Place

New biography was continually available if we could work out how to tap it. Sometimes a photograph would do it, but often it was a sense of place that unlocked Kathleen's stories. We used some of the freedom afforded by Bluebell House to explore old haunts, to play hookey for the day and revisit places that I knew had meant something to my friend in the time before Alzheimer's.

Walking into the famous Saint George's Chapel at Windsor Castle the cool darkness plunged us into blindness. Objects seemed partially formed, distorted by pinprick pupils which still held the glare of the sun. I held onto Kathleen's arm as we stopped by the visitors' entrance, standing to one side of the heavy oak door, pausing to allow time to adjust to the sudden change in light. As we blinked away the sunshine of the Lower Ward, a small functional table emerged, bedecked with leaflets and information. A caped guide sat on a simple wooden chair more redolent of a Victorian schoolroom than a royal chapel; she smiled her welcome and asked if we needed any assistance.

We didn't. It was such a lovely day, we had forgone the tour of the state rooms, preferring instead to walk up the steep hill of the Middle Ward and stand on the North Terrace peering over the balustrades at Eton college, hunkered down on the other side of the river. Kathleen was in her element here. She had volunteered in the chapel for several years following her retirement and she breathed in its welcome familiarity.

On our arrival to the town, Kathleen had been quiet. Such reticence became more usual as her Alzheimer's progressed. When we went out, she needed all her resources just to cope with the change to her routine. In the car, I kept conversation light, pointing out trees, lakes and flowers rather than specific geographical landmarks. This was something else I had learnt to do in the constant accommodation of the disease. Dementia had disrupted Kathleen's sense of place, losing her internal GPS soon after arrival at Bluebell House. Whether the move itself had muddled her inner compass, or whether a natural deterioration would have occurred then anyway is merely guesswork. She still enjoyed the outside world but could no longer identify it reliably. She needed to be encouraged to appreciate being in the moment without struggling to contextualise it. If I mentioned the name of a town or village as we drove through it, her demeanour changed, and anxiety became evident.

'I should recognise this. I've been here before, many times.'

'It's harder in the car. I'm sure you'll be fine once we're parked and walking around.'

Despite my reassurance, it was clear that she was troubled by her inability to resolve where she was. It took huge effort for Kathleen to stay calm and cheerful in the face of perceived failure.

Place cells, our brain's in-built geographical markers, have a particular function in enabling us to remember where we are.[1] These cells, situated in the limbic system, activate as we travel around towns and cities and negotiate our way through buildings and corridors. They act as a comprehensive mapping system, creating spatial awareness and signifying where we are in relation to where we have been. If routes change, our brains re-encode information to keep us on track. During sleep, it is thought that the place cells replay past trajectories in order for our geographical memories to consolidate.[2] Significantly, spatial awareness is a component part of our neuronal circuitry – it underpins key functions of cognition, learning and memory.[3] Brain atrophy is pronounced in the medial

---

1. Eichenbaum et al., 'The Hippocampus, Memory, and Place Cells,' 209.

2. Ólafsdóttir, Bush, and Barry, 'The Role of Hippocampal Replay in Memory and Planning,' 37.

3. Dombeck et al., 'Functional Imaging of Hippocampal Place Cells at Cellular Resolution during Virtual Navigation,' 1433.

lobe of those with Alzheimer's disease and so Kathleen's experience of loss of geographical integrity is commonplace for those living with dementia.

Still quiet as we walked from the car park through the town, Kathleen depended on me for every street and pathway. It is testament to her character that she was able to quieten the anxiety that accompanied getting from A to B – it was another lesson in trust. She could no longer rely on her own place cells, but she chose to trust mine. Every step outside the care home was a living embodiment of her faith in me. Alzheimer's may have weakened her independence, but it had also served to strengthen our relationship.

Once in the chapel, her residual memories of long experience came into play. It has been accepted by psychologists that rehearsal of memories makes them more accessible in the long term.[4] Kathleen was proud of her time as a guide in Saint George's Chapel and it was something she enjoyed speaking about. Experts have also noted that recall is most efficient if we are physically situated in the place where information is initially gleaned. Our memories are fundamentally associative.[5] This was borne out in Kathleen's reaction. The effect of being back in the chapel seemed to reactivate her circuitry and she regained trust in her own sense of place.

'I know this place, don't I?'

'You do indeed.'

'Did I use to work here?'

'Yes. Can you tell me anything about those days?'

Our conversation was necessarily simple. Kathleen's communication was meaningful as long as cues remained short and specific. She didn't need further details from me about the royal church, but she wanted my reassurance in order to be confident that she had accessed a valid memory – it was enough for her to then feel her way into an oft-repeated anecdote.

'I used to wear a sash around my body, like a beauty contestant, to show that I was a guide,' she recalled. 'I began on the entrance desk, here, and then sometimes I would be positioned at different spots in the nave or in a side chapel.'

---

4. Lindeman, Zengel and Skowronski, 'An Exploration of the Relationship among Valence, Fading Affect, Rehearsal Frequency, and Memory Vividness for Past Personal Events,' 726.

5. The Human Memory, 'Memory Encoding | Memory Processes Storage & Retrieval.'

The guide in a red cape rather than Kathleen's remembered sash, smiled at Kathleen's memories and wished us a pleasant tour. We turned left, pausing by the huge double doors at the west entrance, to look up the long nave, towards the organ screen and the quire. Here, Kathleen remembered meeting an 'old girl' during one of her voluntary shifts.

'She just appeared, with no coat or anything, just popped up from that side entrance, by the choir stalls. I wondered why on earth she was there. There was no one with her and she didn't seem to be sightseeing. We were both very surprised to see each other. It turned out that she had married the chaplain and now lived and worked here. Extraordinary!'

Pockets of memory like this were always very specific. They gave Kathleen moments of delight as she retold her own stories with confidence and enthusiasm. Remembering this incident enabled her to recollect the former teacher and chapel guide she had once been. It gave her a brief connection with a past that was getting harder to access, a certainty that she had a significant personal history. Whether the elements of anecdote were accurate is immaterial – as her dementia progressed, it was enough for her to have these windows of clarity.

In the earlier stages of Alzheimer's, Kathleen had been able to articulate her experience of the disease as one of increasing uncertainty and decreasing confidence – it made her depend more on me and Philip and withdraw from those who knew little or nothing of her diagnosis. She feared letting herself down in company by failing to remember basic information, and avoided people who might perceive her to be less than she had been.

Repeated experience of correction and contradiction in conversation with well-meaning friends and family creates a feeling of diminution rather than enablement. Constant editing of your own story by others does more to confirm failure than it does to encourage or stimulate further dialogue. Kathleen's Alzheimer's challenged me to recognise that there are more ways to see and remember than we can countenance. Forgetting is not just a feature of disease – we all forget more than we remember; it is an essential element of being sane, and all memories are subject to revision as we revisit them. 'Memories are no older than the last time they were thought of; there are no *read-only* files. To remember is to create something new: it happens in the present tense, so that in the act of memory old selves are created afresh.'[6]

So, if some facts were a little awry in her autobiographical retelling, it didn't matter. Kathleen, despite the progression of tangles and plaques in her brain, was keeping her narrative alive and gifting me with a glimpse of her former life. She could no longer access her semantic memory for details of tombs, flags and architectural nuance that would have been stock knowledge for her guided tours of the chapel, but she clearly felt at home there and wanted me to share in her enthusiasm.

When we passed behind the high altar, resisting the little shop nestled up against the north choir aisle, and made our way to the exit, Kathleen tensed slightly and looked a little perplexed.

'Are you alright?'

'Yes. I think so. I was Education officer here?'

The shift in her language to include tentative modals and questions made it evident that Alzheimer's was winning – her earlier certainty vanishing as quickly as it had come.

'That's right. You told me you made packs for visiting children.'

This assertion from me was enough to release a memory that had been fuzzy in the seconds before.

'I was pleased when they asked me. It meant I was able to carry on teaching in some way, use the skills I had acquired at school. I made information packs. I typed them up. You could pick them up if you arrived here with a child in tow, or else the school parties used them. I worked hard on them. I remember that. But one day – maybe a change of personnel, I don't know – one day they seemed to say that they weren't interesting enough. I seem to remember a discussion, but I think they stopped using them and I don't think I stayed long after that.'

Such a lengthy discourse was unusual. When we discovered some of those information packs clearing her bungalow in preparation for the move to Bluebell House, she told me a similar tale then too. There was definitely some sadness in her departure from the chapel. Traumatic memory can form the most persistent of human recollection, which suggests that Kathleen may have revisited her

---

6.   Gerrard, *What Dementia Teaches Us About Love*, 69.

departure many times.[7] It is a shame that when we sift our own histories, we can't always lose those that cause us pain.

Despite this, her stories of the chapel were overwhelmingly good, often combined as they were with a tale of when she went to Buckingham Palace for a garden party, 'I went twice, you know.' When she revisited Windsor with Philip, on a day trip organised by Bluebell House, she delighted in telling the guide-on-duty that she had once been in their ranks. She returned home very pleased with the acquisition of a chapel guide pin badge, a gift donated by a stranger who had enjoyed listening to Kathleen's memories. That stranger couldn't have known the significance of her gesture – it enabled Kathleen to own an object that gave her back a sense of her own value, a sense of having had a history and a place. Even with Alzheimer's marching through her limbic system, the badge and her subsequent attachment to it, demonstrated that Kathleen remained fully capable of nostalgia.

The move to Bluebell House shifted Kathleen's sense of place and sense of home. Perhaps pragmatically, she decided that she would be content in residential care, and memories of her bungalow receded quickly. When we turned into the long drive after one of our outings, the sign outside prompted her to ask me:

'I'd never heard of Bluebell House before. Had you?'

'No.'

'Did Philip find it for me?'

'Yes. He got a list of all the care homes and whittled them down to a few. He and Matthew came to visit them and then you got to vet the final shortlist.'

'And have I always been happy here? I don't remember being unhappy.'

I confirmed that she settled in remarkably quickly, and that she was now well-loved by the staff. This was a conversation we had often and like many others of a circuitous nature, had diverging paths to its conclusion. Either Kathleen got righteously cross about the possibility that anyone might criticise the care home or the staff, 'as everyone is so wonderful,' or more commonly, something was triggered that made her uncomfortable, conscious of the holes in her life that Alzheimer's had created. She was often quiet then, as though plucking up courage to ask,

---

7.   Hamann, 'Cognitive and Neural Mechanisms of Emotional Memory,' 396.

'How did I move in, then? Have I sold my house? I don't remember my house.'

One of the aspects of Alzheimer's that can contribute to depression and anxiety for those living with the disease is awareness of their limitations. It is not until the more advanced stages of the disease that someone forgets that they are forgetting things, and though this marks profound loss for friends and relatives, I imagine that it is something of a relief for the person living with the disease. Awareness of her increasing inability to remember was a struggle for Kathleen. She knew she should be able to mine more information than her synapses allowed. She was fully aware that she used to be in charge of her own life.

Here, relationship is what gave me the words. I tried to fill in the blanks whilst reassuring her that she still had much to offer, that her personality was as mischievous, as stoic and intelligent as it had always been. She wasn't lost; it was just getting harder to retrieve some of the pieces that made up her history.

'I can tell you about your house,' I said, and then proceeded to walk her through the bungalow which she had called home for more than three decades.

'Opening your front door,' I told her, 'involved dodging the rather splendid hanging baskets that lined your drive and that you watered religiously. In the hall stood a little wooden bureau with a brass saucer on the top where you kept your keys.'

Kathleen picked up the confidence in my voice and nodded. She still had imagination, even if recollection let her down.

'That wasn't your main desk – that was in the study, near your piano. When we sorted out your house for the move, we found bills in your study going back to the 1970s, all neatly filed. There were hundreds of WH Smith ruled cash books where we could learn about your expenditure on tights, hairdressers and Dairy Milk.'

She laughed at the reference to chocolate. If she couldn't exactly remember the place that I described, she could picture it. I like to think it was comparable to being told a story – intimate, soothing, safe. Home in another sense of the word.

16
Shifting Sands

Bluebell House became home very quickly. Safety of routine coupled with reassurance on-tap meant that Kathleen was able to relax. The care home gave her opportunities that she had not previously had time or space to explore – she made mosaics, painted, played cards and took part in scrabble games and quizzes. Organised by the staff, there was continual accommodation of these activities for those with memory loss; adaptation was achieved with subtlety and respect for residents with dementia.

Studies have suggested that continued mental activity in adulthood can help to retain cognitive function as we age. Rote learning, such as that of the hymns and prayers of Kathleen's past, can be seen to create plasticity in the hippocampus. Vital for memory function, there is some evidence that when new material is learnt and deliberate effort made to commit it to memory, positive metabolic change occurs in the hippocampal region. This evidence for plasticity in mature adults could have significant implications for maintaining brain health in the future.[1]

Such brain training is not fully proven, however, nor is it any guarantee. Kathleen learnt new information for her entire career and enjoyed a stimulating retirement. She did crosswords. She took part in our family quizzes, conferring in theatrical whispers across

1. Roche et al., 'Prolonged Rote Learning Produces Delayed Memory Facilitation and Metabolic Changes in the Hippocampus of the Ageing Human Brain.'

the lounge. All this cerebral activity was not enough to protect her from dementia, but it may be that it stemmed the symptoms. This is conjecture. For now, the best advice for brain health is the same as that for the body – eat sensibly and keep mentally and physically active for as long as possible.

One way I tried to keep Kathleen active was to take her out, away from the safety of Bluebell House and into the real world. I was confident that when she was with me, Kathleen could cope with day trips and afternoon treats. If I'm honest, I relished being her safety net – it made me feel useful and necessary. I enjoyed being able to keep her calm, leading her to places where she could find pleasure outside the confines of the care home.

I knew that before her diagnosis and in the early stages of Alzheimer's Kathleen had experienced anxiety powerful enough to make her believe she was ill. She had cancelled appointments, lifts to church and lunch dates at our house. Since being at Bluebell House, though, Kathleen had been more settled, less troubled. She hadn't rung me to cancel anything for weeks.

I discovered too late that Alzheimer's steals whole days by replacing logical thought with a dense, impenetrable fog. My reading up on the disease came after Kathleen's death. I'm not sure why I didn't rush to the library before; I can only think it was because I felt I was dealing with a person rather than a disease. Commendable though this may have been, I could have done better by the person if I had more fully understood some of the demons of dementia. My knowledge came from hearsay and the media and my understanding of Kathleen. Later research showed me that the days of impenetrable fog mask the world in a swirling mist, where nothing seems reasonable or possible. Even the simplest of tasks becomes monumental.[2] I wish I had understood the extent of the fear that Kathleen must have felt when she battled through such opaque thinking to use the phone and cancel an appointment. As Kathleen had always been a bit of a worrier, I simply attributed it to mild anxiety. And anyway, I was beginning to relax into the routine and safety of Bluebell House; I was confident because Kathleen was confident.

My ignorance was about to be called out.

---

2. Mitchell, *Somebody I Used to Know*, 133.

It was my daughter's eighteenth birthday. Kathleen had been in residential care for four months and I had arranged to pick her up so she could join us for a family tea. I had not yet begun to use the diary retrospectively, so the date was written and circled in red. *Emily's birthday tea. Karen to collect me at 3 o'clock.* When she rang at 2 p.m. to say that she was too poorly to come, I was caught off-balance.

'Oh. But it's Emily's eighteenth. You would love to join in.'

'I would. But I can't. I'm just not well enough.'

The punctuation was emphatic. There was a steel in her voice that spoke authenticity.

'Are you really sure? I could come anyway and see how you are?'

I think I lacked conviction. It was Em's birthday and perhaps I didn't want to go to Bluebell House and encourage and be patient and cajole. Perhaps I just wanted Kathleen to be as she had always been, eager to share in my children's milestones. Perhaps I was just selfish.

'I'll come and see you on Tuesday as usual then. If you're sure?'

'Thank you dear; that will be lovely.'

I tried not to feel guilty. We set up the food and were about to get started when the phone rang again. This time it was the manager of the care home.

'I'm really sorry to disturb you.'

'Not a problem.'

'But we've had Kathleen sitting in the foyer with her coat on for the past half-hour. She is adamant that you were supposed to pick her up, that there's some celebration going on. She's quite upset.'

I explained what had happened. We hadn't cut the cake yet. I was on my way.

When I arrived, Kathleen had moved from her post in the foyer and was in the lounge talking to other residents. They were all settling down for their tea. She was standing next to them, coat resolutely on and handbag tightly clutched, her back towards me. She hadn't seen me come in. Her words rang clearly across the room, raw emotion making her voice loud and brittle.

'I can't believe she would forget me. I'm not supposed to be here. She has forgotten me.'

I stopped in my tracks, swallowing dread that rose from my stomach like bile. She had never been angry with me before. Taking a deep breath, I smiled.

'As if I would forget you,' I called across the lounge, over-bright and a little desperate.

And then she cried. She looked at me and her face crumpled, and she cried. I hugged her and gathered her to the exit. As she dabbed her face with tissues, I tried to explain.

'I'm so sorry, Kathleen. You rang me earlier to say that you felt too poorly to come. I should have come anyway. I'm sorry.'

'I wouldn't have done that. I wouldn't have missed Emily's birthday.' That steel in her voice again, a conviction that I knew I could no longer trust.

She looked at me and must have seen the sadness in my face, 'Would I?' she questioned.

It was her hesitancy that finally undid me, the sinking in that perhaps she might have behaved in a way that wasn't correspondent to her former character. In that moment, at some level, Kathleen understood that Alzheimer's had the power to change her, that the sands had shifted and she could no longer depend on her own version of events. With a watery smile, I tried to reassure her,

'Not usually.' I squeezed her arm and drew closer to her. 'But sometimes this Alzheimer's catches us all out. Don't worry. We'll all enjoy being together for tea. It's Emily's birthday, she's looking forward to sharing it with you.'

And there was no harm done. If dementia has its demons, it also has its angels. By the time we had driven to the bottom of the drive, she had forgotten her distress. She didn't remember the phone call, the waiting or the tears. Once we arrived at my house, she was cordial, composed and greeted my parents with her usual deputy-head-teacher politeness. She congratulated Emily on becoming an adult and ate generous slices of cake. She was herself. I wrote in her diary that she had enjoyed a lovely time.

This marked the beginning of using the diary differently. What had been a tool to ward off memory loss was becoming another source of anxiety. Despite the confidence of the first four months at Bluebell House, if she now read in her diary that I was taking her out for anything more challenging than a coffee, it became inevitable that Kathleen would phone.

'It says here that you are coming to take me out today. I'm afraid I'm not well at all, so can we put it off? I'm very disappointed, but I'm really not myself today.'

I asked Philip and Terence not to tell Kathleen if they were planning a visit. Those dates were instead arranged directly with Bluebell House office staff – the dates highlighted in their diary rather than hers. Alzheimer's had replaced Kathleen's joy in expectation with anxiety and confusion. More tangible proof of memorable loss.

Our weekly collaboration continued, Kathleen in the wing chair and me in its tub twin, the diary open between us on the table. Instead of a means to look forward, it became a trail of proof that she had done more than sit in her room. We wrote down where we had been, what she had enjoyed. I was becoming memory for her, creating an image or impression that her own brain could not hold onto. For a time at least, there was joy in reflective reconstruction of her own narrative.

Following the birthday incident, I never once accepted Kathleen's assertions of illness or fatigue. On the phone, I reassured her that she was probably fine, gently explaining that when she was anxious, she often felt unwell.

'I'll come over to see you anyway. I can keep you company and see if you feel any better.'

On my arrival, Kathleen was, without exception, delighted to see me. She never had any recollection of phoning me and was often ready and eager to go out. Her automatic reaction on my arrival at her door was to gather her handbag and grab a pair of shoes. She associated me with day trips, coffee shops and garden centres. I was her 'escape' as we termed it, though she always called to the staff over her shoulder as she left,

'I might come back. I probably will.'

Eventually, the diary disappeared altogether. Instead of being an aide memoire, it became a symbol of distress, of what she had lost.

'It says here that Philip visited yesterday. Did he?'

When I confirmed his writing and pointed out the fun they were certain to have had, she became quiet and sad.

'I'm sure I did enjoy it. I always enjoy his visits. But I can't remember anything about it. How can this be happening to me?'

Even more distressing was the cycle of grief that the diary caused. When staff at the home learnt of the death of a much-loved former colleague of Kathleen's – her erstwhile Saturday crossword friend – they knew she needed to be told. This friend had been head teacher throughout Kathleen's tenure as deputy. There was a feature in the local paper and it was important that Kathleen didn't stumble on the news.

I wasn't there when they told her, but they reported that she had been shocked, upset and concerned for Jenny's husband. They had been married for over fifty years; how would he cope?

Kathleen noted the date of her friend's death in the allotted Monday in January. She underlined it and circled it. The page quickly became crumpled as the fact of Jenny's death was rediscovered and gained yet another layer of inked circle. Reminiscent of the fearful tears that accompanied continual rediscovery of her own Alzheimer diagnosis some years earlier, this note in her diary elicited fresh, raw grief every time she saw it.

'Jenny has died. My best friend has died.'

Time and time again, her hands covered her face as she sought to take in the news. I held her and tried to give her comfort. Every day when she flicked through her diary, it was there, a bold fact. The date that accompanied it was irrelevant – each time she read it was the first time. Kathleen's short-term memory was lost. There were no cerebral pathways left that enabled her to digest the information and begin to process her grief.

After another repetition, I could bear her pain no longer. We sat in her room, I held her hands and explained,

'Jenny died over a month ago. Because of your memory problems, it is impossible for you to remember that. Every time you read your own note it seems like new grief. She wouldn't want you to keep reliving this shock. She would want you to remember her as she was.'

Kathleen nodded, her working memory able to hold my words just long enough for me to continue,

'If you agree, I'm going to tear this page out of your diary. I promise you that you have cried, you have mourned, you have sent her husband a lovely card and letter. I promise you that we will always talk about Jenny, that we will remember her together, but this note is making you so unhappy. She wouldn't want that.'

'She wouldn't,' Kathleen conceded.

'Can I take the page away then?'

She nodded.

I tugged it cleanly away and pushed it deep into my pocket. It was nearly time for the diary to go.

Together, Kathleen and I learnt to live in the present. If she became anxious about her lack of recollection or ability to handle life as she had once been able to do, I drew her back to now. 'But you are still you. We can have a chat; we enjoy each other's company. You are enjoying your coffee, sitting in this place.'

'I am indeed,' she smiled. 'And I am grateful for that.'

Such simplification could leave me open to accusations of patronising or infantilising Kathleen. I absolutely refute that. Rather, it was recognition of the value of the present, and a reminder to all of us to appreciate what is good in it. There is further benefit to be derived from this; experts have shown that there is a 'striking dissociation' between impaired declarative memory for an event and the emotional experience attached to it, with the emotional response being more important to the continuance of self and wellbeing.[3] Kathleen may have forgotten specific visits made by her brother and nephews, her episodic memory all but gone, but their continuance meant that she held onto the love they had for her. She knew she enjoyed their company. She knew she was loved. Memories of feelings and emotions far outlast memories of detail and declarative fact.

For this reason, we must never underestimate the power of continued interaction, the keeping on, even if we feel we have lost the one we once knew. It is of vital human importance to hang in there, to keep visiting, to hold hands and stroke a cheek, to speak words. When advanced dementia means the past is taken over by a deep black void, we must remember the wealth of feelings, banked and stored over a lifetime. Arguably less tangible than an episodic memory, emotion is found to be more powerful, more resistant to the ravages of dementia. Feelings seem to engage a different part of the brain; they circumnavigate the memory factory of a dying hippocampus, finding a route to the soul. A touch of the hand and a gentle word will engage feelings and let them know that they are loved.

As Kathleen got older and her health complicated by more than the progression of Alzheimer's disease, there were occasions when I saw she was really low, and I made no attempt to cajole her over the threshold of Bluebell House. Instead of focusing on a

---

3. Feinstein, Duff and Tranel, 'Sustained Experience of Emotion after Loss of Memory in Patients with Amnesia,' 7677.

difficult present, we pulled out photographs and took refuge in her past. Her increasingly limited repertoire of anecdotes spoke of an emotional palimpsest that still mattered. The colours and shades in her tone enabled me to better understand the relationships she had experienced with the central players in her life. What they felt for her and she for them had a longevity that dementia never took away.

17
Abiding Narratives

Kathleen quickly came to see Bluebell House as a place where she was regarded with affection. This emotional connection with the staff enabled her to feel a sense of home and family, and although disruption to her place cells meant that she had little idea of where she was when we went out, she always recognised the steep drive and the friendly redbrick manor on our return. Disruption to her episodic memory meant there was little recall surrounding the previous twenty years spent in her bungalow – relying instead on me to fill in the blanks – but Bluebell House became recognisable, dependable, and home. She slotted into a hostess role, responding to years of experience and positive feelings engendered by a return to somewhere she loved.

'You don't have to bother coming in. Just drop me off. I'll be fine from here.'

'I'm sure you would, but I don't want to get into trouble with the staff when you turn up at the door without me.'

I sometimes reminded her that an entry code was needed to get into Bluebell House and she needed my memory for successful re-entry.

'Ah yes. Perhaps you could give me the number?'

On good days, Kathleen was aware of the limits that Alzheimer's had imposed on her thinking and, rather than feel subdued about it, she would try to outwit dementia, or even take it on. Sometimes when she asked me for the code, her eyes twinkled with mischief. It was tongue-in-cheek, an acknowledgement that we both understood that recalling a series of digits was now impossible for her. Occasionally she insisted and we made it into a game. I reeled off numbers and she repeated them, determined to try to persuade her brain that it was still in its capacity to remember. By the time we had walked the short distance from the car to the front door, however, she had no recollection of her request, let alone the code. Such holes in her short-term memory created no distress, because for distress you need access to short-term memory.

What did upset her was the realisation that uncertainty experienced outside the house was beginning to happen inside. Secure in Bluebell House for some years, this marked a sudden change in the neuropathological progress of her disease that caught us both out. Alzheimer's can worsen rapidly, or plateau for some considerable time – it is not a steady linear deterioration.[1]

We walked into the house, now blind to the grandeur that had first impressed Philip, Matthew and Kathleen. The expansive hallway with its panelled wood, lush carpet and a photograph of Theresa May on an official constituency visit were as familiar as the bungalow had once been. The office is situated here, where staff man the phones and keep an eye on who is arriving and leaving. Kathleen often sat in the vestibule to listen to the everyday workings of the house, to chat to the receptionist, nurses and ancillary staff. She was often to be found sitting on the posh sofa with giant red flowers on a plush cream fabric; it was the place she regularly thumbed magazines or stroked the resident cat.

So when Kathleen looked about her and said in a small voice that held none of its previous lightness, 'I'm not sure which way to go,' we were both floored.

It didn't help that, to get to her bedroom, she could legitimately take either the left or right-hand exit from the hallway. I decided from that moment on, we would always take the right. That way, perhaps her neurons and synapses might be able to forge a more reliable pathway. Removing choice might perhaps remove some confusion.

---

1. Bozoki et al., 'The Existence of Cognitive Plateaus in Alzheimer's Disease,' 474.

I guided her through the lounge, keeping my hand firm on her elbow to propel her in the right direction. She seemed diminished, defeated by the extent of the neural confusion that had blanketed her without warning. Willing familiarity to return, I kept up a cheery monologue and waved to residents sitting in chairs around the room. We mounted the 'grand staircase,' as Kathleen termed it – in itself a confusing structure for those with Alzheimer's – its three turns muddling left and right before the landing was reached. At the top I instructed Kathleen to turn left where she could see her door at the end of the corridor.

She recovered her stride then, loosing her dependency on my arm. As her door came into focus, Kathleen injected sparkle into her voice,

'Number 21, my age,' she said, pulling out a standard quip.

The panic in the hall was only momentary, forcing Kathleen to put her trust in my ability to remember what she could not. There was no attempt to cover her confusion; she felt safe admitting her vulnerability to me. Moments like these, when she allowed me to anchor her in her own life, both physically and mentally, was an unsought privilege.

Coat returned to the back of the wardrobe, I stayed with Kathleen for a while to make sure she had fully recovered her equilibrium. *The Times* had been delivered to her room and was poised for a perusal that was becoming increasingly unlikely. Colouring books and pencils were on the table too, and I picked one up and flicked through.

We sat in our matching chairs, still angled to face the dormant television in the corner of the room. Already struggling with familiar equipment in her bungalow before she moved, Kathleen had shown no inclination to master the new one. In any case, I rather suspect that she had lost the ability to follow news stories a long time before. Those living with dementia in its early stages report that film and TV scripts move too quickly for their brains to process. It becomes too difficult to fathom plot and development. For a while refuge can be found in familiar and often repeated programmes but Kathleen had long given up on any form of broadcast. Towards the end of her life, I like to think that she enjoyed being read to, but it was probably more for the company and rhythm of the voice than for any appreciation of narrative.

Once we realised that even the headlines of *The Times* were mere words with no context for Kathleen, we made one attempt to stop the daily delivery. A way to save money, it became quickly apparent that the paper symbolised more than news to my friend. Though she no could no longer use the newspaper to check the date, read the stories or complete the crossword, its absence from her table was immediately noticed. Like playing the piano, Kathleen had no grasp of the fact that she no longer read the paper; she could not conceive of a life where she didn't sit and take in the day's top stories.

We all have props that help us to construct who we are, and *The Times* was an essential one for Kathleen. It was better to keep paying for it than force her to confront a mismatch between self-perception and reality. To the end, she was convinced that she read it every day and completed the crossword over coffee.

In her last two years, in my weekly tidy-up of her room, I found myself recycling barely touched, pristine print. I still have a basket of rescued puzzle pages in my house; each time we reach for one, it is a homage to Kathleen and, even if it remains unspoken, we know it is a good way to remember her. She would approve. Occasionally we find one with a few squares filled in and I rejoice that Kathleen, sitting on her own with her paper on her desk, had experienced a rare moment of clarity, just enough time to retrieve words like *equator* or *glockenspiel*. It is a cruel fact that when we are old, our lexicon, though far wider than most college students, is increasingly difficult to access.[2] When her handwriting speaks across the gulf of months stretching to years, I say hello to Kathleen and have a conversation about her crossword prowess.

'Good effort here, Kathleen,' I say. 'Excellent vocabulary.'

And I imagine her replying,

'Well, you should know, English teacher that you are.'

Sometimes I joke with her beyond the veil of the grave.

'You really should have got this one.' Or, 'Disaster! Even the one you've filled in is wrong!'

And I can see her smile, hear her chuckle, and I am grateful for the shared puzzles and the comfortable friendship we enjoyed.

As I flicked through her colouring book that day, she glanced around the room, her fingers playing with the increasingly worn arm of her chair.

---

2. BBC Sounds, 'All in the Mind – Tackling Mental Health Myths.'

'How did we find this place? Did the boys find it for me?'

Looking back, this oft-repeated prompt would come when Kathleen was tired. We might be sitting quietly in her room or walking up the gravel drive after an outing. In my fanciful reflection, I think she must have internalised some of the narrative. It was, after all, a story that kept Philip and Matthew front and centre of her life, and it was a story with a happy ending, a story worth repeating. At the time I thought that every repetition seemed fresh and new to Kathleen – evidence of the forgetting that comes with Alzheimer's. I'm now unconvinced; in my memory, it seems as though she had simultaneously heard it and not heard it before. Although the episodic detail was missing, proved by her interjections of 'I don't remember any of that,' it was as if at some level she knew what to expect. It was a safe question whose answer made her feel secure in her home and in her family. It was a question that made her feel loved.

Need for narrative seems to be hard-wired into humanity and Alzheimer's didn't override that for Kathleen.[3] Sometimes I would simply tell the story of finding Bluebell House, at other times she would reach into her past eliciting a childhood experience, repeating it as if it was the first time I had heard it, preserving, for as long as we could, her own sense of autobiography.

One of her tales was almost incredible. Prompted by my children taking their A Levels, Kathleen accessed memories of sitting her Highers in a cave beneath her school building in Reigate. A quick perusal of the internet reveals the cave system is still there and very much real.

Kathleen took her Higher School Certificate in the midst of the Second World War. When the air-raid siren sounded, all the girls would have to pick up their books and decamp to the labyrinth of sandstone tunnels and caverns beneath the County School for Girls. Lower forms had to sit on the floor or on benches, but for the sixth form girls, there were chairs and desks.

'We had to have double coats,' Kathleen remembered. 'Even though it was the summertime, it was bitterly cold down there and it was expected that we would all have two coats and a blanket.'

'Was it damp and dreary?' I wondered, conjuring up grey stone walls with rivulets of water running down to the cave floors.

---

3. Rose, 'The Art of Immersion.'

'Oh, not at all. I don't know how they did it, but it was actually quite cosy. There were separate classrooms and they even had flushing toilets down there.'

Pauses often punctuated Kathleen's narrative as she relaxed into a memory – the march of tangles and plaques reducing her capacity to make connections, to tell her story fluently. Scaffolding narratives with questions and encouragement was a way to keep her autobiography alive.[4] I learnt to read the silences, judging whether to prompt, wait or take over for a bit.

'What happened when the alarm sounded?' I asked.

'The siren would go off and utter silence would fall. Not a sound from the girls. I don't remember any panic or hysterics. We simply stood up, gathered everything and walked in single file to the caves. The steps were steep, but handrails had been added. Remarkable really, when I come to think of it.'

As someone who endured university exams with streaming hay fever, Kathleen declared herself grateful to the bombers who enabled her to take her Highers in a pollen-free zone.

The war did not rage in leafy Redhill, and Reigate was never a target, but they were en route from the capital back to Germany and were vulnerable to Nazi ammunition-dumping during the Blitz. As a policeman, her father's duty had to be to the neighbourhood as well as his family. Kathleen told of a 'rather serious discussion' around the kitchen table.

'Now,' she reported him saying, 'I need you to know that whenever the air raid warning goes off, I'll need to leave you all. We need to discuss what you are going to do.'

Three alternatives were offered – he could build them a shelter in the garden, as many of their neighbours were doing, he could clear the cupboard under the stairs so that the three of them could squeeze together on a mattress there, or they could do nothing. Kathleen was adamant that it was she who first found her voice.

'If I'm going to die, then I want to go to heaven from my bed and not a bunker.'

And so it was decided. Kathleen, her mother and brother, Terence, would defy Hitler by sleeping through the Blitz.

Kathleen spoke of her father with pride. Alongside the story of the shelter, she often followed up with this detail,

---

4. Schiffrin, Fina and Nylund, *Telling Stories*, 150.

'He was in bomb disposal during the war, that's why he was never at home with us.'

Although it is indeed true that policemen had many additional responsibilities during the war – first the call came for reservists, many of whom were in the police, and then wider conscription, leaving the force depleted and ageing – I haven't found anything to suggest that they were involved in the intricacies of de-activating or detonating unexploded devices.[5] Here we see evidence that Kathleen's memory was not always reliable. She, like all of us, modified her own experience, created her own heroes.

At eighteen, bombs notwithstanding, Kathleen passed her Higher School Certificate, proving the worthiness of a scholarship won whilst at St Matthew's Primary in Redhill. I asked her whether she had ever considered that going to university as a woman in the 1940s was pretty exceptional.

'No. Though I suppose it was, in a way. Thinking about it, there weren't many girls who went on to university. I had two great friends, they were twins: Norma and Leila. They had been all the way through school with me and we were as thick as thieves. They didn't go to university. Only I did as I recall. They did that job ...'

Here her words got lost. Characteristic of Alzheimer's from its earlier stages, sometimes evident in the pre-clinical phase of mild cognitive impairment, is the vacuum where vocabulary used to be. Psychologists term this retrieval difficulty as *tip-of-the-tongue* and it is experienced universally. When we are young, we hardly notice it, but as we get older, there is a tendency to regard such lapses with dread, fearing its collocation with Alzheimer's.[6] In the process of normal ageing we can expect a doubling of tip-of-the-tongue phenomena, but the steady decline in linguistic function associated with dementia often results in more pronounced anomic aphasia.[7] To overcome such loss of vocabulary, often failing to find verbs and nouns, those living with the disease often circumnavigate specific lexis by an increase in generic description.

'They did that job that you do to get limbs working again after an accident.' Kathleen spoke around the word she was trying to find, pointing me in the right direction.

'Physiotherapy?'

---

5. Open University, 'Police at War: Second World War.'

6. BBC Sounds, 'All in the Mind – Tackling Mental Health Myths.'

7. Schiffrin, Fina and Nylund, *Telling Stories*, 149.

'No, the other one. They show you how to do things.'
'Occupational therapy?'
'Yes. That's what they did. Occupational therapy.'

Born in a traditional household where her mother wasn't allowed to go out to work, Kathleen's desire to achieve her ambitions marked her out as different. She equated marriage with a lack of freedom, believing that it would force her to give up any thoughts of a career. She sacrificed desires for love and family in order to teach.

When I visited Exeter University as a prospective place for my son to study, it felt like a bit of a pilgrimage. Hope Hall, where Kathleen lived as an undergraduate, is still there. I made sure that there was a photo of me in front of the sign so that we could see if she recognised it.

She didn't, but the picture was enough to evoke memories of taking turns to sit at high table with the masters and mistresses, with boyfriends allowed to accompany the girls only on selected days. Although never hers, she laughed at the awkwardness of these young gentlemen when having to fit into the formality and rigour of an all-female institution.

Her first job was in Maidenhead County School for Girls, and Kathleen arrived in 1950 to take on the role not just of teacher, but head of Geography. This steep trajectory was not without cost. She admitted to breaking down and weeping in front of her father that first Christmas holiday.

'He gave me permission to give it up, to jack it all in. He knew how hard I'd worked and how long I had wanted to be a teacher, but he was letting me know that first and foremost I was his daughter, and my happiness came first.'

It seems to me that moment was the one when she realised how much her father loved her. It gave her strength, she says, to carry on,
'and I'm forever grateful that I did. I have never regretted the years I spent in the classroom.'

All these stories were gleaned from moments in the present that took Kathleen back to a remote past that she could remember. Taking refuge in personal narrative has been seen as a regression in Alzheimer's disease, a withdrawal from the real world. But it can be viewed differently, positively, as a creative solution to retain fragments of a life, helping those living with dementia make sense of their life story and hold onto identity.[8]

8. Schiffrin, Fina and Nylund, 150.

18
Language of Consent

Kathleen's ability to access her repertoire of personal narratives remained more or less intact until her final weeks. Detail was lost as she got older and the dementia more advanced, but the central stories remained.

Her eloquence was preserved, fitting the common experience of language being resistant to substantive decline until the mid to later stages of Alzheimer's disease.[1] This is not the case for all people who have been diagnosed with dementia – some move rapidly from commonly experienced anomia, the technical term for word-finding difficulty, to aphasia, where production and comprehension of language is much more impaired.[2] Variation in linguistic competence is dependent on the extent of degeneration evident in the left side of the brain, in the frontal, temporal and parietal regions – thus more severe impediment in language use is seen in vascular and frontotemporal dementia.

Despite persistent language skills, Kathleen found initiating conversations difficult. As the disease progressed, she became quieter, increasingly reliant on cues and context to provide framework for meaningful communication.

1. Memory and Aging Centre, 'Speech & Language.'

2. Marczinski and Kertesz, 'Category and Letter Fluency in Semantic Dementia, Primary Progressive Aphasia, and Alzheimer's Disease.'

Polite speech is predictable, following adjacency pairings that have been rehearsed over a lifetime of conversation, so a generic 'How was your morning?' would elicit a sequential reply, 'Lovely, thank you.' No detail followed, no recollection, because there was none. If the question was more specific, 'Where have you been this morning?' Kathleen retained the intellectual skills to answer cogently, with a 'here and there,' but similarly there was no memory to access particular information relating to the recent past. From early on in her diagnosis, I found that specific temporal or recollection questions caused only muddle and confusion, resulting in distress. Better-framed questions provided a much more effective scaffold for meaningful conversation. If the cue became, 'How was the dentist?' she was able to reply with confidence and humour, 'Oh wonderful, thank you. One of my favourite ways to spend a morning!'

I am certain that when my husband asked her this question, Kathleen did not remember any details of the visit we made together on a damp December morning in the final months of her life. It is left for me to remember that, for the first time, she was too frail to climb the stairs and that the dentist was kind enough to decamp to a ground floor surgery. She didn't remember that, for the first time, I had to instruct her to bend her legs in order to sit down, or that I had to interpret everything the dentist said to her because the experience proved so overwhelming that it rendered her incapable of even the most basic response to an unfamiliar voice.

Decades of visits to that particular dental practice enabled Kathleen to answer my husband, to mask her loss of specific recollection with a general and genial response. To a casual observer, there would have been little to point to the total absence of short-term memory.

This mask did not always work, and it is right that it didn't. It is right that as a society we are exposed to the effects of memory loss and learn to become better at dealing with it. For us, any attempts at collusion and outwitting Alzheimer's came to a full stop when other medical issues became prevalent. Though Alzheimer's disease is terminal, it is often not the primary cause of death. Because many of those living with the disease are elderly, they are vulnerable to many corporal failures. Like her mother before her, Kathleen was suffering from anaemia which hadn't been resolved or much improved by standard medication. It became necessary to move up from the GP and visit a consultant.

Until this point, Kathleen's medical appointments had been straightforward. Philip and Matthew had medical power of attorney as well as financial, so all was in place should difficulties arise.

Autonomy is not easily relinquished, however, and consent not simply overridden by the holding of a legal document.

Kathleen had always trusted doctors and taken their advice to heart. Following knee surgery early in her retirement, she responded to instructions to climb stairs daily by catching a bus to town and going up and down the flight in Marks and Spencer's. She had no stairs in her bungalow, so it was the 'only way to do as the doctor suggested.'

Faced with an endoscopy to determine whether her anaemia was being caused by a bleed in her small intestine, Kathleen was happy to consent to the investigation. I drove her to the hospital and went into the consulting room with her. Living with Alzheimer's for almost a decade now, she was still able to answer transactional questions.

'Your name?'

'Kathleen Barr.'

'Date of birth?'

'December 29th, 1927.'

'And your address?'

There was a pause. The nurse's pen halted, and Kathleen looked across at me. I supplied the name and details of the care home.

'Of course.' Looking towards me, Kathleen continued, 'I don't know what I'd do without her.'

The nurse clerking us in, smiled, before asking,

'Do you know why you are here today?'

Kathleen looked to me again. I took the appointment letter out of my bag as a prompt and explained the fact that she had been getting tired lately and the doctor thought an endoscopy would be a good idea.

She nodded and confirmed that she understood all that.

Once details had been added to the form, the nurse asked Kathleen again, very gently,

'Do you know why you are in hospital today?'

Kathleen smiled at the nurse as she tried to compute the answer to the question. The uniform conferred authority on the younger woman, and Kathleen was programmed to respect that, to comply and give the expected response.

It was evident that she couldn't do that anymore. She didn't have the answers. Her face dropped and she looked again to me, as if willing me to take over. I indicated the letter and repeated my explanation.

Kathleen was showing the typical memory pattern of someone with Alzheimer's. She was able to immediately register and understand information presented to her, but this was only transient. The thirty second window of working memory was fine, but there was no embedding of salient information.[3] Was this enough to consent to an invasive medical procedure?

Capacity to consent to medical treatment is a fundamental aspect of personal autonomy. From a functional standpoint, it is regarded as one of the advanced activities of daily living. From a conceptual standpoint, it is more complex – being able to have competency to make informed medical choices involves the application of four different consensual standards. The first demands that a person has capacity to evidence a treatment choice – this is the most basic level of consent, and looks to see whether a person can understand that there is a decision to be made – it is not concerned with the quality of the decision. Ability to make a reasonable decision is subjective and therefore cannot form part of the standards. To overcome this, professionals are asked to examine whether their patients are aware of the effects of a treatment – its emotional impact and consequences. The evaluation of risks and benefits is used to assess rationality. Finally, a patient is assessed for their ability to understand the treatments being offered. This last process is predicated on memory for words, phrases and sequential understanding.[4]

A person living with Alzheimer's might well be able to meet the first standard – Kathleen's immediate understanding of the need to make a decision was evident – but the consequent demands are much harder.[5] In testing ability to give informed consent, research indicates that those with Alzheimer's will experience significant impairment.[6] The Mental Capacity Act 2005 gives clear guidelines about making a decision on behalf of someone else – it must be in

---

3.   Attix and Welsh-Bohmer, *Geriatric Neuropsychology*, 58.

4.   Attix and Welsh-Bohmer, *Geriatric Neuropsychology*, 172–5.

5.   Attix and Welsh-Bohmer, *Geriatric Neuropsychology*, 174.

6.   Wong et al., 'The Capacity of People with a "Mental Disability" to Make a Health Care Decision.'

their best interests and, where possible, take into account previous knowledge of the patient.[7] With this in mind, I assured the nurse that Kathleen would have given assent and that if there was any difficulty, to refer to her nephews who held power of attorney.

To enable the procedure to take place, Philip was phoned and a conversation ensued between him and the consultant. For now, that was sufficient, and the endoscopy went ahead. I wasn't allowed in the treatment room – something I found difficult. Who would translate for Kathleen and have the patience to keep explaining what was happening? I was brusquely reassured by a nurse and ushered into the waiting area.

Hospitals are not readily dementia-friendly. Despite good intentions they are often short-staffed and short of time. This was my first experience. Should I have insisted that I be allowed to accompany her? Was she distressed as the procedure took place? Was the kindly nurse of my imagination holding her hand and talking her through it, or is that just a story I tell myself?

Given that I felt Kathleen needed me with her, then I probably should have fought harder to be allowed in, but both Kathleen and I are conformists; we avoid conflict and comply readily with received convention. I rationalised the decision all the time I was sitting in the waiting room, trying to quell a strong sense that I had abandoned my friend. The doctors, I told myself, would have performed this procedure hundreds of times on other elderly and vulnerable patients. These people made it their life's work to care for others. She would be fine. Kathleen had undergone worse things on her own before her diagnosis, so she would simply follow instructions. But all the logic in the world didn't make me feel comfortable. At some fundamental human level, leaving her in the care of strangers felt wrong. I clocked it up to another notch on the Alzheimer learning curve and knew I would behave differently next time. Whilst having no desire to silence Kathleen or decide for her, that appointment showed me the necessity for a trusted advocate, someone who can best and most faithfully represent the person with dementia when they cannot be fully autonomous. This was a gut response that went beyond anything offered by the legal paperwork of power of attorney.

---

7.   Alheimers' Society, 'Alzheimer's Society's View on Decision Making.'

Life doesn't work neatly, and I couldn't attend her second outpatient's visit. I was studying for a Masters, and that day I needed to be at Warwick University for tutorials. Kathleen understood this prioritising of education, of a prior commitment, but she was now limited to the timeframe of her working memory. She endorsed my decision in the moment of our conversation,

'Of course you must go, dear. You can't miss lectures.'

And I had to be content with her blessing. If she was confused when the appointment came and I wasn't there, then I would never know. Her advocate for the follow-up procedure would be Shirley, her care home nurse, by now a loved and trusted extension to Kathleen's family. I knew she would be fine.

To Kathleen, I was always a teacher. She didn't remember that I had left school in order to take a year to study. She never fully computed that I was doing an MA, or that for two days each week I was out of circulation. Her reply demonstrated a strong unspoken sentiment that she never wanted to be a burden, a reason for me to curtail any aspect of my life.

The next step in trying to find the cause for Kathleen's anaemia was more invasive, and I was conflicted about the wisdom of subjecting her to it at all. She was approaching ninety-two and significantly frailer than in previous years. Philip was contacted and, using his knowledge of his aunt, had consented on her behalf. If Kathleen understood that there was a possibility that a colonoscopy could sort out the anaemia, then she would certainly have opted in; of that he was certain. It had the potential to make her feel much better, less lethargic and more herself. We felt confident that Shirley would be able to advocate, probably far better than me. She hoped that her medical credentials might qualify her to stay with Kathleen throughout the procedure.

In the end, the consultant refused to give Kathleen the more invasive colonoscopy. He decided that even with the support of her own nurse and the power of attorney in place, she lacked capacity to make an informed choice. Her impairment in short-term memory meant that she would certainly forget why such a procedure was being done – it was not pleasant, and she may be frightened or panic. It was imperative that she remained still during the procedure – sudden movements could result in catastrophic damage. There were no guarantees that the process would result in positive diagnosis or treatment. In his view, it was in Kathleen's best interests to leave well alone. His objectivity and experience were the best basis for deciding consent.

I visited Kathleen at Bluebell House the following day. In my opinion, uninformed and unmedical though it is, the effects of the preparative treatment for the colonoscopy were devastating enough. With its prerequisite dehydration and starvation over a period of twenty-four hours, Kathleen had become incredibly confused and disorientated. Shocked at her sudden deterioration, I found myself in full agreement with the consultant – Kathleen didn't need to be put through any more investigations.

The ongoing medical care of someone living with Alzheimer's shifts as the disease progresses. Kathleen had made several transitions – from total autonomy, to increased reliance on me, then deferring to Bluebell House staff, until finally she rescinded all control, depending on the triumvirate protections conferred by power of attorney, a Do Not Resuscitate (DNR) order and the knowledge and compassion of medical staff to ensure her best interests were met.

Philip and care home nursing staff were joint gatekeepers in Kathleen's decision to sign the DNR a couple of years after she moved to Bluebell House. The management of the home felt that Kathleen retained capacity to understand the implications of such an order but also had the foresight to recognise that this was unlikely to be the case further down the line when such a medical directive might be needed. Philip was called in and there was a meeting. Consent was handled with absolute integrity – the DNR was explained and Kathleen was asked if she wanted to sign it. Looking at Philip, she replied,

'Are you saying that when the good Lord decides my time has come, medical staff could intervene to prevent my going to heaven?'

He told me that he'd held her hand as he held back his tears.

'Yes, I suppose so. If you stop breathing, doctors will try to revive you unless a DNR, this form, has been signed.'

'Then what are we waiting for? I don't want to be late for my appointment with God.'

Shared faith meant Philip understood her conviction. A profound moment for him, he was relieved that all those present at the meeting recognised that Kathleen had full understanding of the implications of the DNR. Despite the confusions and muddles associated with Alzheimer's, Kathleen remained certain that death was not the end of her story.

Her stoicism, humour and practicality made such decisions more bearable for Philip and the family. When the consultant advised against the wisdom of a colonoscopy, however, it was still incredibly hard to accept that, without it, the only choice left was palliative care. Something was causing Kathleen's persistent anaemia, but we would never know quite what.

Here the tables turned. Whereas it had been Philip who had been certain about the decision to move Kathleen into Bluebell House five years previously, now it was me who was certain of the rightness of the decision to scale down medical intervention. The distance that had given clarity to Philip before, now obscured the heartbreaking reality of what was a sudden decline in his aunt's capacity to cope with the demands of life.

It was me who witnessed her sudden deterioration following the non-event of the colonoscopy – it was plain to me that even the preparation for the procedure had been way too much for her. Dehydration had exaggerated her confusion, and with increased confusion, anxiety and fear engulfed my friend. She needed calm reassurance and companionship far more than she needed a cure.

I expressed these concerns to the matron whose judgement I now trusted implicitly. She agreed with me and said that if it were her mother she would not consent to further treatment. She made a phone call to Philip, and his confidence in her medical opinion was enough.

That visit to the dentist on a damp December morning turned out to be Kathleen's final outing with me. I am glad we returned via my house, even if it served to underline the fact that the walk down my garden path was costing her a colossal effort. It meant that she sat at a family dining table and had coffee and biscuits 'in a real home, part of a family,' something she had appreciated all the more since moving to Bluebell House. A pause in work calls meant my husband had time to join us, to share his affection for this lady who had impacted our lives more than we could have imagined.

19
The Narrowing Gate

It was from this point that she began to stay in the confines of Bluebell House. Our coffee shop visits dwindled to nothing and it was as much as Kathleen could do to get dressed and go downstairs. Her horizons no longer needed to be wider than the care home; she just needed to be loved in a place where she felt safe.

She was increasingly tired and frail in the weeks that followed. Staff at the care home were on alert for any changes, and I was called in several times to hold her hand, reassure her and keep her company. Every time the phone rang, I steeled myself. Their experience was telling us that Kathleen may not have much longer. Philip came down with Terence, knowing it was likely to be for the last time. Matthew visited with his family, and I began to visit my friend every day.

Alzheimer's meant that she remembered nothing of these visits. She welcomed the company for a short while before she got too tired and then she slept. For the first time I saw Kathleen as the very old lady that her nine decades had formerly belied. Too weak to be bothered to eat, I would coax her with soup and bribe her with ice cream. No matter how lethargic she became, ice cream never lost its joy for Kathleen. And there were windows of opportunity – the photo albums came out again and we remembered together, using all the old stories to comfort her. Occasionally she would grip my hand and ask,

'What is happening to me?'

She complained that she couldn't see properly, that nothing made sense. It was as if she could feel her former sense of self drifting out of reach.

'Where am I?' she asked as we sat in the room that had been her home for more than five years. 'What are those things?'

'What things?'

She indicated the direction of the window.

'There are animals in my house. I don't like it.'

'There are no animals. It's just you and me in your lovely room.'

I wish I had understood the visual disturbances dementia can cause. I didn't know that eyesight could be affected, though I suppose it's logical really. Tangles and plaques disrupt neurological function. The optic nerve sends signals from the eye to the brain. Dementia disrupts those signals, obstructs them, renders them something other than they were before. Anything can be affected if you have the disease long enough.

Looking back, it seems clear that Kathleen had lost all depth of vision as the Alzheimer's fought to do battle with the anaemia and come up with new symptoms of its own. Outside her window was a green field, dotted with sheep. With little sense of perspective, it may well have felt like they were in the room with her.

I simply held her hands and tried to distract her. I positioned myself at her eye level, filling her field of vision with me in the attempt to turn her foggy mind to something immediate and now.

'You're just a bit discombobulated at the moment, that's all.'

I reached into her personality and out to her knowledge of me.

'Discom what?' she said.

'Discombobulated. It's a great word for confusion, don't you think?'

She smiled then, and turned to the care worker in the room,

'You can tell this one's an English teacher. She's always trying to teach me long words.'

We all laughed, spending a joyful few minutes away from invading sheep whilst Kathleen focused on trying to get her tongue around the new word.

Moments like these didn't take away the most distressing symptoms of these weaker weeks and months. Increasingly, Kathleen experienced hallucinations that made her impossible to reach. Hallucinations are commonly associated with declining cognitive function and are experienced by over a third of those living with dementia.[1] Kathleen began to see her grandfather and her parents; she would reach out to them and tell them, 'No, not yet.' To me, it seemed as though her loved ones were calling her home, but she wasn't ready. Their appearance did nothing to comfort her; she became agitated and distressed. When she spoke to them, her voice was pitched higher than normal. Kathleen became someone I didn't fully recognise, and I found these episodes very difficult to watch. The real world receded, and I could not get through. Talking to Kathleen had little or no effect. In the end, I just stroked her hand and prayed for it to stop.

Later reading taught me that the experience of hallucinations feels very real; being pulled back to the present can cause further distress. I learnt that my instinct to ride the vision was probably the right one. Living with dementia and educating others about Alzheimer's, Wendy Mitchell writes that 'the helpful response is probably to "go along" with our experience. It's not unethical to do that; it's just valuing the person's experience.'[2]

This was easier said than done. When Kathleen was seeing her parents, she would stiffen all over and reach out to thin air. Her body took on a strength it didn't have in normal life. Her distress robbed me of the capacity to do anything other than murmur a reassurance that I was certain she could not hear.

During a spell in Accident and Emergency, her hallucinations took on a more darkly comic content. Struggling to sit up, she spoke with exasperated impatience to the vision of her grandfather,

'No Grandad, not a dog. You can't get a dog,' her voice was firm and admonishing, a remnant of the former teacher.

'You tell him, Kathleen,' I said encouragingly, looking with some irony at the ward we were in, 'it's just not practical right now.'

My mother-in-law had hallucinatory visions associated with Parkinson's disease, and she told of funeral processions outside her window and a monkey in her room. Protected by the fact that she wasn't my mother, I was able to go along with her visions, enter her world for a few minutes. My husband hated every moment, desperate to pull his mum back into the real world. Watching a

---

1. Wilson et al., 'Hallucinations, Delusions, and Cognitive Decline in Alzheimer's Disease,' 172, 176.

2. Mitchell, *Somebody I Used to Know*, 193.

loved one interacting with something ethereal is like witnessing them slipping away. It is not surprising that, at times, the urge to persuade them back to reality is overwhelming.

Exhausted by the simple effort of life, even the walk along the corridor and downstairs to the lounge in Bluebell House became too much. Kathleen began to take all her meals in her room. Eventually, even the ten steps from her chair to the bathroom took Herculean effort, and she needed someone to support each arm to prevent a fall.

The cruelty of Alzheimer's disease was all too apparent in these weeks. Stoically independent, her sense of selfhood was compromised less than her short-term memory. If she needed the bathroom, or to stretch her legs after 'so much sitting,' then she saw no reason not to get up. She consistently refused a wheelchair. It was only when she tried to stand, that she realised such simple activities were no longer possible without help. Once re-seated, however, the extent of her exhaustion was veiled and so she tried again, repeatedly. Memory impairment was making life dangerous for Kathleen. Buzz mats were installed round the room to alert staff if she was on the move.

In these days, I struggled. Sometimes I battled with my conscience, torn between deadlines associated with my MA – it was only a year after all, and I wanted to make the most of it – and the persistent feeling that I should visit every day. When my tutorials were later in the afternoon, I popped to Bluebell House in the morning on my way to the M40; when they were earlier, I made a pit stop at the end of a day in Warwick. My faith helped me here. Even if I didn't want to go, I knew it was the right thing to do, and I prayed that Kathleen would never see any of my inner conflict. Without exception, the visits were worthwhile. Even if she was tired and too weak to chat, she would open her eyes every few minutes and squeeze my hand.

'I didn't know you were here,' she repeated each time she roused.

Her pleasure at seeing me, even if for the most part she was unaware of me, was enough. I needed her to feel loved. I hope I succeeded in communicating to her that she was.

There were some moments of wonderful relief when the old Kathleen resurfaced from the exhaustion created by the dual battery of Alzheimer's and anaemia. A wry grin or a raised hand; a 'see you later, alligator' to the staff as they left her room allowed us all to realise that she was still with us. A photograph of the two of us by the River Thames prompted memories of a holiday she had taken on the Broads in her student days, where conversations carried across the water, amplified in the stillness. She was with me for a minute or two, smiling and remembering before tiredness or confusion overwhelmed her; then her head nodded to her chest, too heavy for this world.

I don't remember the moment when she stopped getting dressed. I know that Shirley, her key nurse suggested I buy Kathleen a cosier dressing gown than the now thin green velour that we had lovingly packed nearly six years ago. I wondered why I hadn't thought of this myself – perhaps I hadn't accepted that her days of getting dressed were over. The lighter housecoats that Kathleen had insisted on bringing were no longer warm enough for her thinning frame and so I bought the softest, warmest one I could find. I bought her new slippers for her birthday late in December, slippers that were still pristine when we returned them to their box some two months later. I don't remember when she stopped sitting out in her chair and spent all hours in her bed. There isn't a moment. It's just a continuum. I prayed I would be able to find the right words, the right tone, to be who she needed me to be. I visited and she slept. I read to her or prattled on about everything and nothing, punctuated by increasingly frequent visions of her long-dead relatives. Sometimes I would arrive to find her sitting on the edge of the bed. She had swung herself out and was ready to go but wasn't sure where. That happened a lot.

And then she broke the neck of her femur. No one is quite sure how. She had probably decided to get up and stretch her legs, forgetting her infirmity. Maybe she just stood up and her fragile bones snapped under the weight of the effort. All we know is that staff found her perched rather awkwardly on the bed. She wasn't crumpled in a heap on the floor, she didn't cry out for help. Quietly, stoically, Kathleen merely sat at an odd angle, stranded like a starfish on her own bed. Standing her up to sort out the tangle of bedclothes, a nurse encouraged Kathleen to put her hands to her blue-uniformed shoulders and walk a sidestep with her. That's when she heard the click.

'I knew I needed to call an ambulance as soon as I heard it,' she said to me on the telephone. 'Can you come?'

I could. I jumped in the car and checked the time. 10 p.m. The call to the emergency services had been put through before they rang me. I should be able to make it. I raced to Bluebell House, determined to arrive before the ambulance. I didn't want Kathleen to face this confusion on her own. She needed me.

She needed someone. A care home worker or nurse would have been perfectly fine, but I needed to be there for my own sense of … And here I lose words. It wasn't a sense of duty that compelled me. What was the force that meant I knew it had to be me? Looking back on the longest night of my life so far, I can see that it was love, pure and simple. Kathleen had become family and I loved her. I now trusted the staff completely; they were deeply fond of their long-term resident, but I needed her to know that she was with someone who loved her.

None of those thoughts were in my head as I drove through the dark, twisty lanes leading to Bluebell House. All I knew was that I had to be there when the ambulance arrived.

I beat the blue lights by about ten minutes. Kathleen had been laid back in her bed by the nurses and was completely fine. There was no confusion or distress, just a wry bemusement that there were so many of us in her room in the middle of the night. My adrenaline levels dropped. She was fine. As long as she didn't try to move, she had no memory that anything was amiss. Alzheimer's has its benefits at times of trauma.

I threw some bits and pieces in an overnight bag and persuaded Kathleen that as it was a while since we had been out, then this was simply another adventure for the two of us. It would be more exciting than the dentist.

The ambulance crew arrived. Ascertaining that Kathleen was both frail and living with dementia, they reassured her whilst addressing any medical or technical questions to me or the staff.

'She is a highly intelligent woman. Please explain everything you are doing to her,' I urged. 'She won't remember what you've said, but please tell her anyway.'

Even with the expertise and compassion shown by this crew, they interpreted my request with a list far too long to be cognisant to a person with Alzheimer's.

'Now Kathleen, we think you may have broken your hip, so we are going to slide you onto this bright yellow scoop. We'll do the left then the right-hand sides and then clip them together. We'll need to stabilise your legs so that movement is reduced …'

They spoke clearly and directly to her, seemingly unaware that it was impossible for her to hold so many sub-clauses together. Standing at the foot of her bed, out of effective earshot for me to be of any practical use, I felt desperate that Kathleen wouldn't be given a chance to understand what was happening.

'One instruction or explanation at a time will work well,' I explained.

They let me station myself at her head and I let them work. I became her interlocutor.

'You've hurt your leg. We're taking you to hospital.'

'They are going to slide the scoop under you. It is going to hurt. Ready? The yellow scoop is to help you out to the ambulance. Here it comes.'

Kathleen's personality shone that night, as though the quiet confusion that had enveloped her in recent weeks had never been. She liked being the centre of medical attention. She rediscovered her sense of humour, at one point taking my phone and reassuring Philip that she was fine.

'Karen and I are off on an adventure, apparently,' her voice clearly holding laughter in its tones. 'You're not to worry. I have some very handsome men to look after me.'

I added my reassurance. She was coping well. I was happy to go to the hospital and stay for as long as it took. He should try to get some sleep and come down in the morning. No need for him to do a mercy dash in the middle of the night. It would be fine.

Now I realise that as well as trying to be kind to Philip, I wanted to be Kathleen's person that night. In a remnant of the days before Bluebell House, my saviour-complex had kicked in and I needed to be the one. I needed to be useful again.

Her legs now tied together with medical strips (stabilising the hips is pretty rudimentary), Kathleen was manoeuvred onto what looked like a full-size Duplo stretcher, Chris the paramedic came into Kathleen's full view to give another instruction,

'Right. Now I need you to cross your arms over your chest, like this.'

She obediently conformed and then looked straight at me. In a moment that now seems suspended in time she asked, straight-faced,

'Are they measuring me up for my coffin?'

The room lost its buzz for a moment. Everyone there knew that hip injuries were often the last straw for the elderly. But this was Kathleen – my friend with the driest humour and raw talent for satire,

'Maybe just a tad premature,' I retorted.

There was a pregnant pause in the room as the ambulance and nursing staff looked at each other and then towards me and Kathleen. I caught Kathleen's eye and we all laughed.

Dark humour, maybe. But it was a hallmark of her character and a trait of our friendship. Kathleen had forgotten the fall that caused the paramedics to be there, she only remembered her broken body when prompted by the pain of movement, but in that moment she remained fully in touch with her identity.

20
Holding On

The stereotype that feeds widespread fear associated with Alzheimer's is that dementia will steal character and rob families of their loved ones. It has been described as a living death.[1] This bleak view is one that focuses on loss rather than on what remains. More positive discussions of dementia recognise that personality persists long after recall is dramatically impaired. Proponents of the ideology of living well with dementia often draw a distinction between the cognitive self, which is hugely disrupted by memory loss, and the sentient self, which is not.[2] Even when dementia is at its most advanced, people will respond to smiles, hugs and handholding, even more so if accompanied by a familiar voice.[3]

Personality persists, but it seems likely that lack of episodic memory precludes those living with the condition from fully recognising limitations imposed by their impairments. It is not unusual for people with dementia to underestimate their age and thus overestimate their competencies.[4]

The functioning self who has always managed personal affairs, driven a car, paid bills, run a home is more quickly deconstructed by

---

1. Peel, "'The Living Death of Alzheimer's" versus "Take a Walk to Keep Dementia at Bay,'" 88.
2. Gearing et al., *Mental Health Problems in Old Age*, 133.
3. Segal, Qualls and Smyer, *Aging and Mental Health*, 167.
4. Eustache et al., 'Sense of Identity in Advanced Alzheimer's Dementia,' 1,15.

the disease – the effects of memory loss make daily living impossible to perform reliably. For safety, many of those living with the mid to late stages of dementia are cared for in homes or by close supervision in their own environments. In 2013, Alzheimer's Research UK published figures that showed 39 per cent of those with dementia aged over sixty-five were living in care or nursing homes, whilst a further 61 per cent lived in the community reliant on care provided by family members or caring organisations.[5]

Elements of cognitive deficit that result in inability to retain independence can lead to a despairing acceptance that Alzheimer's is indeed a 'very real dismantling of self.'[6] This idea leads into the realms of philosophy, prompting examination of what it is that defines us. If we are to see ourselves as more than the sum total of what we remember, then we need to be able to recognise key components of identity that are retained when neurons and synapses are slowly destroyed. In tests to establish the persistence of a personality, those living with dementia in various stages from mild to advanced were asked to affirm or deny statements such as *I am honest, I am serious-minded, I am cheerful.*[7] Right up until her death, Kathleen had a clearly preserved sense of who she was. Reflecting on our friendship, we discussed the fact that we had rarely disagreed with one another and never argued.

'I would hate it if we did,' she stated quietly, summarising her deep-rooted aversion to conflict. This is who she was, and who she remained until the end. Even though her articulation may not have been what it was, she retained a hold on her intrinsic 'I am.'

Key to Kathleen's 'I am' thread was humour, and this was evident even through the pain of a broken hip. Other Bluebell House residents helped me to see their 'I am' selves through card games, singing and other activities. Joan was quick to tell visiting handbell ringers that this was not something she wanted to listen to, 'When on earth are they going to stop? Who is going to make them stop?!'

But humour is rooted in the present. It is quick-witted commentary on life as it is. After the quip about the coffin, Kathleen became quiet. She shifted a little way from us as hallucination once more muddled the boundaries of time.

---

5. Dementia Statistics Hub, 'Care Services.'

6. Davis, 'Dementia,' 378.

7. Eustache et al., 'Sense of Identity in Advanced Alzheimer's Dementia.'

'We're going to move you soon,' said Chris, the senior paramedic.
'Move me where?' Kathleen's eyes flitted around the room, her voice taking on a brittle edge.
'To hospital, Mrs Barr, where they'll put you right.'
She strained against the straps that held her to the plastic scoop.
'I can't go. The girls are all waiting for me on the third floor. I can't leave them. They're expecting me.'
This was a new one for me.
We could only assume these girls were her pupils, the like of which she had not taught since 1984. In her mind, she was younger, capable and responsible. I joined in with what I assumed Kathleen was seeing.
'Someone else is looking after the girls.'
'No. It is my job. I can't leave them.'
'No, Kathleen. Jenny knows you are poorly, and she has gone to the third floor.'
I hoped that by citing Jenny, Kathleen would have the confidence to rescind the responsibility that she believed to be hers. Jenny had been head teacher to Kathleen's deputy role. She had also died two years before this. But at this moment, Kathleen was firmly stuck in her notion that she was still a teacher. Her identity – that of consummate responsibility – was embedded beyond the vagaries of memory loss.
Reassured that she could leave the girls with Jenny, Kathleen allowed the paramedics to do their job. The effort of moving her from the comfort of her bed to the floor and down the twisting staircase precluded everything but the pain of the present. There was no space for humour or hallucination, just endurance. Bewildered and hurting, fear crept over Kathleen's features and settled there. As they manoeuvred her into the waiting vehicle, I was instructed to stay outside until she was safely installed. With the doors firmly shut, I shivered into the January night and hugged my arms around me.
Standing with Bluebell House night duty staff, there was little conversation. My visits had always been in the daytime, and I didn't know the shift staff well. We threw each other smiles now and then, a silent acknowledgement that reassurance would have been meaningless. We all knew what a broken hip could mean to a frail old lady.

It makes a difference when it's your frail old lady – even when there are no blood ties. Mounting the steps to the ambulance, I was instructed to strap myself into the little seat opposite Kathleen. Health and safety meant I couldn't stand next to her pallet for the journey, couldn't keep myself in her view. Tightly strapped to the gurney, Kathleen was unable to move her head to face me; she could see nothing other than the roof of the ambulance. I twisted in my chair, willingly awkward, so that I could at least place my hand over hers. I spoke to her calmly for the painstaking forty minutes that took us through dark and twisting streets. Kathleen was quiet, her silence punctuated only by a beseeching refrain for the ambulance to stop.

'We're on our way to hospital. They will look after you there. It will feel better soon.'

The paramedic had warned me that the journey would be painful. After examining Kathleen, he had shown me that her right foot hung about an inch lower than her left,

'This is a tell-tale sign of a fracture. I'm not a doctor, but I'm as certain as I can be that her hip is broken. She will be in the sort of pain that you can't imagine, every time she moves her leg.'

It stands to reason that every pothole, every speed hump in the road was excruciating. I kept up a litany of reassurance, telling her I was there, using my name so that she could hold onto a sliver of context.

'It's okay. Karen's here. I'll stay with you.'

'Nearly there now.'

'You're doing so well. Karen is here. You are never going to be on your own.'

Once we'd arrived at Accident and Emergency, Chris, the paramedic drew me to one side.

'You may have noticed I kept quiet on the journey,' he said. 'Kathleen is scared. Your voice made a difference. Mine only added to her confusion. Keep with her; keep doing what you're doing. It makes a difference.'

He squeezed my shoulder as he left us in the hands of the triage team. I would remember his words in the coming weeks, as Kathleen lost strength to speak or react – I would try to keep on talking.

Accident and Emergency is a disorientating environment even for those of us with full cognition. Lights are always on – there is no separation of day and night. Nurses, doctors, porters and auxiliaries buzz around, the weight of the next thing to do bearing on their gait. We were scooted in and white curtains were whisked round Kathleen. She was cold and shivering, shock of the fall was beginning to do its work. A kindly uniformed woman noticed her distress and brought us more of the thin blue NHS blankets. I tucked her in and stroked her cheek.

'We're in hospital now. Soon the doctors will be able to check your hip.'

Kathleen was overwhelmed. She couldn't remember falling, she had no pain because once she had been taken out of the ambulance and bundled to the bed, she was still; her legs were strapped together, and she couldn't move. She didn't understand why she was there. Confusion was evident in her face and she kept her eyes locked on me. I explained repeatedly and simply where we were, why we were there and that she was safe.

The last time I had been in A and E had been for grit in my daughter's eye. I had only been in an ambulance once before and that was when I had snapped my ankle bone clean in half decades before. My experience of hospitals is mercifully little, but my experience of Kathleen was enough for me to know what to do. Love found the words and kept her panic at bay. Focusing entirely on Kathleen, I parked any sense of dread at what the next chapter in her story might be.

21
A Gift

Triage was swift and we were moved into the windowless ward of A and E central. This was a place of eternal waiting – for X-rays, consultants and admission. It was noisy, an irregular rhythmic blend of machines beeping, alarms going off, feet intent on destinations unknown. Cries of pain were punctuated by aggressive, frustrated tones, accompanied by bass notes of chesty coughs and the unmistakeable percussion of guttural heaves. It made for an unpredictable and lonely soundscape. Dignity was left behind at the doors as strangers ministered to the most basic of needs; privacy was only that afforded by the thinnest of curtains.

In the middle of all this noise, of all these people, we were left alone to manage as best we could. Kathleen was in bed with the blue blankets tightly tucked around her. I stood at her bedside, stroking her hair back from her face, murmuring more reassurance.

'They'll be with us soon. We're waiting for an X-ray on your hip. We're in hospital. I'm here. Karen is here.'

Whilst I recited this circular litany, I kept an eye on the end of the bed, watching staff as they bustled past, brisk and efficient. Everyone we met that night was kind, but they had clearly learnt the art of averting their eyes as they skirted the curtained cubicles. They knew we all needed them. They were doing all they could.

As far as the system was concerned, Kathleen and I were sorted. After a speedy triage afforded by our ambulance arrival, we were clocked in and assessed. There was nothing for them to do until the X-ray had been taken, and no time for staff to care any more than that. They don't have the resources to explain to and comfort a patient with dementia who will almost certainly be confused and disorientated. Advocates are a necessity here, and I was grateful that this time it was me.

'I'm very cold,' Kathleen admitted, clutching the covers in her hands.

'I know. You've got lots of blankets. I'll come nearer to you to share my warmth.'

'I can't seem to move my legs.'

'That's because they are strapped. You've hurt your hip and you're in hospital to sort things out.'

Articulating her discomfort exhausted her, and Kathleen became quiet.

I placed my warm hand on her cheek and spoke quietly to her, willing her to get some rest. I resisted the urge to keep looking at the clock. It didn't matter what time it was or how long it took. We were in the right place.

The jolt of the bed being unlocked startled Kathleen.

'What's happening?'

'Hello. Sorry about that. Did I wake you up?' A porter grinned at Kathleen as he expertly shifted the bed out of the bay.

'This is the porter who will take you to X-ray,' I explained. I threw him what I hoped was a meaningful look, as I went on, 'It's okay. I'm coming with you.'

He nodded at me, signalling his understanding. I wanted to stay with Kathleen and that was fine by him. He pushed the bed swiftly along the curtained corridor, through the noise and competing demands and through a heavy set of double doors. As soon as they sucked themselves shut on A and E, an oasis of quiet descended, wrapping us in welcome calm. Suddenly all I could hear was the slight crunch of bed wheels on a wipe-clean floor. Our destination, despite the strip lighting, was a place where it was allowed to be night. The reception desk was unmanned, primed with files ready for tomorrow. Only one radiographer was on duty. There was no queue. Metal blinds were closed on the coffee shop. Most of the people who worked here were at home, asleep in their beds. The tension I had felt in the cubicle lessened and I stretched my arms, flexed my shoulders. Kathleen was silent and still. It was as if she had surrendered to unknowing, no longer asking why or where or how. The porter parked us in a wide aisle outside X-ray. We'd be called in by the radiographer and then he'd be back to collect us later. Smiling at Kathleen, he wished her all the best.

We were seen almost immediately. The system for night X-rays was efficient – the only clients were from Accident and Emergency, and they were brought up in strict turn. Restricted by medical webbing holding her legs still, I was concerned that Kathleen would be unable to be manoeuvred for the procedure.

'That's fine,' the radiographer said, his voice kind and gentle. 'She can stay in her bed and I'll slide the plates under her; then I'll move the camera where it needs to be.'

As he disappeared behind the lead screen, I followed him.

'Can I stay with her? She has Alzheimer's and this is all very bewildering.'

'Of course. But you'll need to come behind the screen when the X-ray is being taken.'

The quiet of Radiology seemed to have seeped into Kathleen's consciousness. Her earlier fear and confusion were replaced with pliant conformity. I talked her through each stage, explaining why her legs were so uncomfortable, and helped her to shift into the positions needed for the image. The radiologist was surprised that the emergency binding used by the ambulance crew was still in place but explained that it needed to be a doctor who removed it. Kathleen instinctively tried to stretch as she was moved for the camera; she yelped, surprised by unfamiliar pain.

'Try to stay still. We think you took a tumble getting out of bed at Bluebell House. You might have done something to your hip.'

I shied away from saying that it was likely to be broken. It seemed like an admission of fatality – those over sixty-five who suffer a hip fracture are three times more likely to die in the year following the accident than the general population. Not as straightforward as it first seems, this statistic is made complicated by the fact that those most vulnerable to falls often have pre-existing medical conditions such as dementia, Parkinson's or heart disease, thus it is difficult to fully discern the significance of the fracture against subsequent rates of death.[1] Kathleen had pre-existing conditions of Alzheimer's

1. Panula et al., 'Mortality and Cause of Death in Hip Fracture Patients Aged 65 or Older – a Population-Based Study.'

and anaemia. I felt that to voice what the ambulance crew had been pretty certain of, was like telling Kathleen that her time had come.

Looking at the digital images, the kindly face of the radiologist looked grim.

'I'm sorry to say that your friend is going nowhere without an operation – a break that bad needs surgery.'

I had been resigned to the likelihood that Kathleen had broken her hip, but in my ignorance hadn't reckoned on surgery. Looking back, it seems astonishing that my mind failed to admit the possibility of an operation. Everyone I had known with a hip fracture had needed surgical intervention. Tired and naïve, I now think that my brain was protecting me. To look into the future was too bleak; I was existing only in the minute we were living in. Nonetheless, I was completely blindsided by his words. Surely no one would advise putting Kathleen through that ordeal. She was ninety-two, anaemic and frail; even a colonoscopy had been deemed too intrusive for her to cope with. How would she ever survive anaesthetic? It was the early hours of the morning and I felt as though I'd been punched.

'At her age?'

'Not my place to decide, but look at it.' He pointed to his screen where, even to my untrained eye, the break was unmistakeable. 'The head of the femur, the ball, is totally sheered from the bone.' He dropped his voice to the level of a secret. 'She won't even be able to sit up without being in agony.'

My face must have reflected the dread I was feeling.

'I'm sorry. She is a lovely lady,' he said.

He pushed the bed out of the X-ray room himself, smiling at me before he turned to the space we had previously vacated in the corridor. Someone else needed his care.

We waited by ourselves in the vast white space. Heavy doors to the radiology areas ensured we could hear nothing from inside, and the absence of a porter meant we were to stay put until someone came to take us back to the hubbub of A and E. It was absolutely silent, ironically serene. I stood next to Kathleen who had stopped shivering for the first time since we arrived, and I stroked her hand. In that moment, there was only us in the world.

Lying back on the bed, wrinkles of nine decades' experience smoothed back, she looked younger than she had for weeks. I tucked the white hair that she had been told would never go grey – redheads never lost their colour – back behind her ear. She turned her palm to take my hand in a firm grip.

'I don't quite know how you arrived in my life,' she spoke with a conviction that came from deep within, finding articulation for the first time since we had got into the ambulance; 'but I thank the Lord for you every day. I don't know how I would have managed all of this without you.'

My eyes fill every time I remember this. My throat thickens and I feel the pressure of her hand on mine. With my free hand, I touched her cheek and told her she was much loved. I told her what a blessing she was to my family, and how much her own family loved her. And then she closed her eyes and drifted into a light sleep.

Tears spilt down my cheeks as I looked down at Kathleen. I thought of Philip, and wished he had seen his aunt so peaceful. I wished he was with me. I felt privileged and guilty that I had wanted to be the one to lead her through this trauma and that I had urged Philip to get rest, to drive down in the morning rather than racing through the dark midwinter night. At the same time as I wanted him there, I prayed too that she might slip away before decisions needed to be taken, that she might be spared the horrors of an operation or the pain of living without one. That she might never realise that even sitting up was impossible for her now, that her life, already complicated by dementia and anaemia, was about to be further reduced.

That moment was a gift. The last real conversation I had with my friend. My final window into her beautiful and generous character.

22
Complications of Consent

Beauty is often fleeting. That moment, which I will treasure for as long as my own memory allows, was a few minutes out of a very long night. It was not yet time for her to slip away. She needed to say goodbye to Philip; he needed to be able to say goodbye to her. Pushed back into the bustle of Accident and Emergency, Kathleen shifted into several hours of agitated hallucination. We were parked back in our cubicle, this time needing to consult with a doctor before being transferred to orthopaedic admissions.

Each time Kathleen hallucinated a remembered loved one from her childhood, she attempted to sit up and reach out to them. The effort cost her; pain emblazoned itself across her face as her hip flexed against the movement. She slumped back on the pillows, arms still outstretched to Grandad, to Mummy and to her dad. The repeated movements shifted her towards the edge of the bed, until the only thing stopping her slipping to the floor was my body, wedged up against her. Trying to prevent her from falling at the same time as trying to soothe her from the agitation of her visions, I was becoming stiff and anxious, fighting rising panic and yet trying to remain calm, reliable and dependable. The early hours of the morning were beginning to take their toll on me. I felt a bit sick. Kathleen's hallucinations had never gone on this long before. She had no idea I was even there. I stopped talking, putting all my energy into bracketing her to the bed, trying to keep her from moving against the fracture. Eventually I managed to get attention from a passing nurse who helped me to move Kathleen gently back to the middle of the bed. As she pulled up the cot sides to protect her further, she smiled at me. I fancy it was a rueful, tired smile, an apology for the lack of bed rails after the X-ray, and an acknowledgement that they were doing the best they could. Released from my position, I was suddenly engulfed by the claustrophobia of noise and activity. Kathleen was lost in her own world and I needed to get out.

I poked my head into the neighbouring cubicle, apologising to the family gathered around their sick teenager. I explained to the nurse that I needed the bathroom, and could she keep an eye on Kathleen, before I paced it to the end of the ward, if it can be called a ward, and locked myself in the disabled loo. It was the first one I came to; I don't know if others were available elsewhere. This was a hospital; maybe all the facilities were accessible. I sat there with my head in my hands and wondered how I would get through the rest of the night. It was nearly 3 a.m. and I was all Kathleen had. I wanted to be what she needed, but in that moment, I doubted my ability to find the resources. I was tired, Kathleen was likely to be facing a major operation that she wouldn't be able to consent to, and I couldn't soothe her out of the longest round of hallucinations I had witnessed. Scrubbing my hands under the tap as if I were a surgeon, I uttered prayers that I had little conviction in. Dread at returning to the noise, the desperation, the utter uselessness that I felt, swamped me. I leaned my head against the cold mirror and reminded myself to breathe. Panic threatened to take over, beginning in my brain or my belly, I couldn't tell which.

Stepping back, I looked at my reflection. Mentally, I pulled myself together. I told myself that I didn't feel sick, I could cope. I was in a disabled loo. I knew it was wrong for me to be in there too long. I had grabbed a few minutes of escape and now I had to go back. Kathleen needed me.

Miraculously, the consultant was at the bedside when I returned. The first of my frantic prayers, answered. Guilty that I had kept him waiting, he assured me it was fine, but that he'd seen Kathleen's X-ray and she needed to be admitted. He wasn't going to operate tonight, but she would be on the list tomorrow if we decided to go ahead. I garbled an explanation about power of attorney not being mine to give and that Philip was travelling down first thing in the morning.

'Will he be here by 7?'

'Probably not. He's ...'

'He needs to be here by 7. That's when I'll come round with the anaesthetist and decisions about the day's surgery will be taken.'

I gave him Philip's number with no real hope that he might have time to call. Ringing Philip myself, I realised the irony of my earlier advice that he should get a good night's rest. Phone calls at 3.30 a.m. were not going to be conducive to sleep. I brought him up to date and asked him if he could be here by 7. He could. He would grab a cup of coffee and get in the car now. It would be best for Kathleen if he was there. It would be best for me if he was there.

Transfer to the orthopaedic ward was surprisingly rapid after all the waiting. The movement of the bed trundling through dimly lit corridors had brought Kathleen back to us, but the absence of visions was not replaced with calm. She was scared and disorientated. I had no certainty that she knew me, so I deliberately used my name.

'I'm here. It's Karen. I'm staying with you. You're in hospital and you're safe.'

I didn't tell her it was going to be fine. None of the options were fine.

Given her own private side ward and asked a gamut of questions she couldn't answer, Kathleen became increasingly distressed.

'She has Alzheimer's,' I explained quietly.

Asking me to leave the room for a moment, they transferred her to the bed. I winced at her shrill notes of pain. Placing pillows at her head so that the angle of her hips to her body was no more than twenty degrees, they set about removing the ties around her leg and inserting a catheter.

'Sorry about that, my love,' the nurse said to me as they let me back in. 'She'll be more comfortable now. That was a long time for her legs to be strapped.'

I sat in a blue faux leather NHS wing chair next to Kathleen's bed, and welcomed the sudden quiet and darkness. Positioning myself so that my head could rest against the wing whilst my arm tucked in next to Kathleen's, I was grateful no one had asked me to go home. Another answer to prayer. I couldn't bear to leave her. Calmer now, and chatting softly about nothing, I talked her to sleep. It was a deep sleep induced in equal part by trauma and the painkillers she had been given. Her breathing was deep and very slow, and suddenly seemed awfully finite. Several times I held my own breath, waiting for her to exhale and repeat. Occasionally she yelled out, more often to Grandad but occasionally to her parents. Like a mother, I soothed her.

'Karen's here. You're safe,' I repeated as I stroked her paper-thin skin and watched the clock tick us back into daylight.

Philip's 6 a.m. footsteps were welcome ones. Immediately intuitive, he dropped a gentle kiss on Kathleen's sleeping features and murmured his arrival. We hugged one another, not something we had done before, but we both needed the comfort of the other. Seeing that his aunt wasn't going to rouse, he sought out the matron and got an update. He came back into the room and we exchanged whispered detail of the night before; he explained that they'd let me stay because I was able to keep Kathleen quiet.

'They already had a couple of dementia patients who were calling out. They could see you were good with Kathleen and decided that it would be most helpful if you could stay. They just don't have the staff.'

That's why I hadn't been ushered home once she had been transferred. I was grateful for their pragmatism, thankful that the duty staff on the orthopaedic ward that night had recognised that living with Alzheimer's would make Kathleen's experience of hospital disorientating. Compensating by flouting visiting rules and letting me stay, they took the trouble to look after me as well as Kathleen, bringing me a blanket for my chair and furnishing me with tea and a croissant during the breakfast round. They had a dementia questionnaire, asking me to highlight Kathleen's preferences and capabilities. What did she like to be called, what food might she be persuaded to eat? I offered it to Philip to fill in, but he deferred to me. He loved his aunt but knew I would be more up to speed on the details of her everyday life.

Consent had already proved difficult in regard to endoscopic and colonoscopy procedures. Today's decision was much harder. With the injury, Kathleen's capacity plummeted. Since her return to A and E, she had barely spoken other than to cry out in pain or in hallucinogenic visions. She showed no sign of understanding where she was or why she was there. All we got was an occasional faint smile when Philip or I spoke to her. She was unable to reach even stage one of legal consent – the ability to recognise that a decision needed to be made. This one was entirely on Philip.

The consultant was honest and direct. Contrary to my expectations of the night before, he had found the time to ring Philip. On this ward round then, he was merely repeating information that he had spoken down the phone in the early hours.

'Your aunt will probably never walk again, with or without the operation. You say she has been increasingly frail of late, and struggling to get across the room?'

Philip nodded.

'She can't get across her room on her own anymore,' I added quietly. 'She needs a person on either side of her to support her.'

Kathleen's weakness had come on so quickly. Although I had been in regular communication with Philip and he had been to see her several times since the non-event of the colonoscopy, the truth of just how weak she had become in recent days was hard to take in.

'Her anaemia complicates things too, I'm afraid,' the consultant went on.

We spoke over her bed. Now, I think we should have discussed all this outside her hospital room, but we didn't want to leave her. We assumed she was asleep or too out of it to comprehend. I hope that was the case.

'With the operation to repair her hip, Mrs Barr will be able to sit up.'

All medical staff assumed Kathleen's title was that of a married woman. Whenever we had any appointment, Kathleen corrected them. That day, I let it go.

'With her recent history,' the consultant continued, 'she isn't suddenly going to improve and be able to walk unaided, but, if she survives the operation, she would be able to sit up, to be taken out in a wheelchair.'

'Given her age and her medical conditions, there is also a risk that she might die on the operating table. No one wants that for their loved ones,' the anaesthetist added.

'We'll give you some time and pop back.'

Philip looked dreadful. He knew it was his call. We both knew that, had she had full capacity, Kathleen would always trust medical advice. She would take the pills, do the exercises. But there was no clear path here – on the one hand the operation was essential for any quality of life, on the other, she was already ailing and there was a risk that the very operation she needed would be too much for her to take. When asked what they might do if it was their mum, both the surgeon and the anaesthetist were kindly pragmatic. There were no easy answers, but the surgeon said, inevitably, he would err on the side of surgery. The anaesthetist was more guarded. It is ghastly to lose someone on the operating table was all he said.

Seeing her sleeping, taking slow shuddering breaths, it was clear that she was in no position to help Philip make the decision. That's why she had appointed him her power of attorney. She trusted his judgement.

'I don't know what to do,' he said, his voice thick.

He looked away from the bed and out of the window onto a barren patch of old gravel peppered with weeds. He wiped his face and then turned to look at me.

'Neither do I,' I admitted.

Fighting tears, we took Kathleen's hands in ours. I was so glad it wasn't my decision. Neither option was desirable. Nothing would rebuild Kathleen to what she had been.

The thought of putting her through an operation was horrible. So was the idea of her not having such a bad break repaired. They had confirmed that without the surgery, Kathleen would be bed-bound and unable to be raised up beyond twenty degrees – high enough to facilitate sipping liquids and have food spooned into her mouth. She would need to be moved regularly to avoid bed sores. The words of the paramedic bounced around my brain, *You cannot imagine how painful a break like this is.* We knew the unstable fracture would mean that with every shift of position Kathleen would experience searing pain, and Alzheimer's complicated it even further. With no context for the pain, it would be even harder to bear.

The palliative care team were very helpful. Pain, they assured Philip, could be managed should it be decided that the operation was too risky. Would the care home take her back? Many don't once a major fracture has occurred.

'She can't die here.' Of that Philip was certain.

A call to Bluebell House reassured him that they would love to have Kathleen home. She had lived there more than five years. Their nurses would be privileged to care for her.

That clinched it. With phone calls to his wife, Matthew and Terence, Philip was able to say that he thought it best to let Kathleen go home, to be in the place she had come to love and where they had come to love her. She would be taken home to die.

Decision made, he then implored me to go back to my house and get some rest. It was now nearing midday; I had been on shift with Kathleen since 10 p.m. the previous night. It was his turn now. He would stay with her, seeing her safely back to Bluebell House before coming over to stay the night with us. Nodding, I came around the bed to give him another hug.

Stroking her cheek as she slept on, I said goodbye to Kathleen, told her Philip was with her now and that I would see her tomorrow.

23
Tomorrow

Tomorrow turned out to be different in every way. The return to Bluebell House was more complicated than anyone had envisioned.

I wasn't there for any of this. After waiting until nightfall before Kathleen's need for hospital transport moved to the top of the list, Philip was already tired. Hospital days are long, and Kathleen had remained asleep while he sat with her and dozed and waited. For the journey back to Bluebell House, Kathleen travelled in the ambulance on her own. Philip had been assured that she was totally cared for, that she would know nothing of the journey. Heavy-duty painkillers had been administered. Following their lead through the dark back roads, he prayed the pills would be enough and that she wouldn't feel scared or abandoned.

I wasn't there when, farce-like, realisation dawned that they couldn't get Kathleen safely back to her room. The transport ambulance was not an emergency vehicle; it wasn't equipped with a narrow scoop, and theirs could not negotiate the turns in the stairs at Bluebell House.

It was awful, Philip explained. She was parked in the entrance hall for hours as they tried to find a solution. It was getting late. I received a text message saying that he had no idea how long it was going to take and that we shouldn't wait up for him. Was it possible for us to leave a key where he could find it? They needed to get Kathleen comfortable at Bluebell House before other residents saw her like this in the hall. They all wanted to protect her dignity. Unspoken was the knowledge that she would never want to be seen strapped helplessly to a stretcher, her mouth slack with drugs and sleep. Philip remained adamant they shouldn't, couldn't return to hospital. After the agony of the decision to bring her home, reversing it seemed impossible. Staff agreed. This was Kathleen's home. It was where she needed to be.

Eventually, a room swap with a ground floor resident was organised. She willingly made the move, roused from her own bed to accommodate Kathleen. Now Kathleen would live downstairs at Bluebell House, near the staff room and the central lounge.

It was nearly midnight before Philip's key turned in my front door.

It was odd, seeing her somewhere else. Back at Bluebell House the following morning, we stood quietly in the room off the dining area as Kathleen slept on. The new room was darker, smaller, narrower. It should have looked onto the garden, but there were building works there that winter and so bright orange plastic cordoned off where the patio was being redone.

'We need to make it hers,' Philip said.

It was difficult not to recall Kathleen's clapping delight as she walked into Room 21 for the first time all those years ago. That couldn't be repeated. But still, we could do something.

Kathleen slept deeply, and Philip and I had work that needed to be done. We set about stripping down her old room, its new resident compliant in spending the day in the lounge so that we could take away Kathleen's things and move them downstairs. Only we didn't need to do that. We realised that she would need very little of what made number 21 home. As if he had been expecting to clear out at short notice, Philip procured cardboard boxes and cases from the boot of his car. He looked at me half-apologetically,

'When you said she had definitely broken her hip, I wondered if we might be needing these …' he trailed off.

'It's good that you were prepared,' I said.

We filled them with none of the careful lists and propriety we had shown five years before. Instead, we were trying to imagine what the rest of her life might look like, what she might need or appreciate.

'Her shoes? She won't need them anymore, will she? She's just going to be in bed.'

We talked to each other, in part to convince ourselves of what had just happened. Twenty-four hours ago, she had been weak, but fine. There had been definite Kathleen moments amid the exhaustion and the hallucinations. Now we spoke of an invalid who needed to be washed, fed and cathetered. We weren't certain if she would ever emerge from the deep sleep that was protecting her from pain.

'You're right. Put them in the pile to go.'

'She's only had these slippers a few weeks,' I fought emotion as I returned them to their box. I had given them to her for her ninety-second birthday, the box wrapped in deliberately obvious paper with *Happy Birthday* emblazoned on it. She had no concept of the date or its significance to her. We were keeping face in the battle of advanced dementia.

'What about all her clothes? Will she be dressed or only in nightgowns?'

'Put them in the suitcase. Just keep bed socks, nighties and a few cardigans for the new room.'

This was really hard. It was as if Kathleen had died already; we were clearing out her room and putting clothes in boxes destined for a charity shop, and yet she was just downstairs, a few metres below us. It felt like we were intruding, prematurely dismantling a life before she was ready to go. So much of her room was testimony to Kathleen's enduring sense of self – her coats and shoes, her colouring books and pencils, notebooks and pens. There were magazines and those pristine copies of *The Times*. There were books she hadn't opened since her arrival and the John Stott biography that she had begun over and over again beside her bed.

We kept a couple of photo albums to put on the shelves in the new room. Maybe she'd wake up enough to have a look at them with me. We moved her Wedgewood glass snail and elephant to the windowsill downstairs and kept the framed photos of family for the new coffee table. I filled a box with her toiletries and included her lipstick and face powder. Maybe …

But really, we both knew. Kathleen was a very poorly lady. She was an old lady with a broken hip and anaemia and Alzheimer's. Already on palliative care, we knew we had brought her home to sleep her way to heaven in a smog of medication. We knew that the albums would stay in a drawer; the lipstick would remain on a glass shelf in a bathroom that she would never get to see.

Tears were shed. There was laughter too, as we found a stash of chocolate with various use-by dates. We unwrapped some of it and imagined her wry disapproval as we ate a couple of chunks as our lunch. Then we found a crumpled piece of paper with familiar print in blue biro.

'No! I can't believe that she still remembered this and wrote it down.' Philip worked hard to control his emotions. He wanted to explain.

'She gave me a copy of this poem years ago. She said it might help me. I used to give it to my staff. This just sums her up completely.'

Philip began to read aloud and just about got to the end.

Somebody said that it couldn't be done
But she, with a chuckle, replied
That maybe it couldn't but she would be one
Who wouldn't say so – til she tried.

So she buckled right in with a trace of a grin
On her face. If she worried she hid it.
She started to sing as she tackled the thing
That couldn't be done, and she did it.

There were thousands to tell her it couldn't be done;
There were thousands to prophesy failure;
There were thousands to point out to her one by one
The dangers that wait to assail her.

But she buckled right in with a bit of a grin
Threw off her coat and got to it;
Just started to sing as she tackled the thing
That couldn't be done, and she did it.[1]

'I have to keep this,' he said through his tears.
'You do.' I gave him a hug and passed another tissue.

---

1. Poetry Foundation, '"It Couldn't Be Done," by Edgar Albert Guest.'

24
The End

Snow is beautiful, but it is its silence that strikes me with each fresh fall. Busy sounds of life recede to nothing. Birds stop singing; cars are kept at home as everyone hunkers down and waits it out. Dare to go outside and the silence is audible, a muted world waiting for something yet unspoken to happen next.

The sky was leaden with more flakes and the fields covered in virgin whiteness. Sporting a chaos of woollens, I ventured out with a friend and her long-legged lurcher. It was the same friend who had assured me Kathleen was fine all those years ago across a crowded church hall. We were the only two people walking the invisible footpaths across the farmland and through the woods. The dog was overjoyed, leaping and bounding through the snow. We talked little and laughed a lot. It was freeing to be out here where everything was the same but different. We took winter selfies and walked on up the hill.

At the top was a bench. Nicely situated to see across to Windsor Castle and Cliveden Manor when the skies were clear and the sun shone. Today, it was hard to distinguish between sky and land. The horizon was blurred, and boundaries muddled. We didn't try to sweep the inches of snow from the slats that I knew to be green. My friend was going to wait here so I could pop down Spring Lane and visit Kathleen. I said no. Visits were much shorter these days, but

I didn't want to keep her and the dog waiting in the cold. Movement was needed to appreciate the beauty of it all.

I had cried on that bench. Since bringing Kathleen back from the hospital, tears often welled and spilt as I walked away from Bluebell House and down the drive. Dashing them away as I walked back down the lane, I sometimes stopped at the bench and let it all go. When it all seemed too much, I phoned loved ones. My daughter took early lunch breaks to walk the hospital perimeter where she works, so that she could chat to me, make it seem better.

Philip had said his goodbyes the day we sorted Kathleen's room. We hugged each other as he left, acknowledging that he was saying the bigger farewell. He was leaving his aunt to the care of the staff at Bluebell House. He couldn't ask for better. It was what she would have wanted. I was to let them do their job, he insisted. He didn't expect me to stay there or visit every day. We would speak often. Together but apart, we would both wait on Kathleen's timing.

Matthew and Terence had said their final farewells once the palliative decision was made. Others visited to say their goodbyes: Jill, who had regularly walked up the hill to Bluebell House to bring Kathleen the church newsletter and point out its highlights; a couple from Oxford who had visited occasionally and sent many cards and letters. Her former life had largely slipped away before her. Some had died or become too infirm themselves to keep in touch, perhaps others were too nervous of what Alzheimer's could do.

The staff rallied around, wanting to administer to Kathleen, to make these final days easier.

Kathleen never acknowledged that she was now downstairs, in an unfamiliar part of the house. Her surroundings became meaningless as she slept most of the time, her glasses useless on the bedside table. They had taken out her hearing aids too, so that they wouldn't become uncomfortable as she lay flat all day. To speak to her, I sat near the head of the bed, holding her hand, and leaning in to talk. I tried to hold onto the assurance of the staff that it was worth talking. Though Kathleen seemed unconscious of anything around her, hearing is one of the last senses to give up. She could hear me, they reassured. She would hear me and know that she was loved.

On that snow day, I crept into Kathleen's room as quietly and inconspicuously as my wet outdoor clothing would allow. She could be easily startled if I came in too breezily, her deaf ears giving her no warning that anyone was approaching. Such startled jumps caused her pain, and we were all very careful as we entered her room.

She was in that limbo between wakefulness and sleep. Her eyes were open and blinking, and yet her breathing indicated deep rest. I can only imagine that her world was one of permanent snow – quiet, muffled and strangely unfamiliar.

Peeling my layers, I apologised for the pools of water gathering on her floor as the melting flakes dripped from the coat I had hung on the back of the different wardrobe.

'It's snowing,' I said, trying to puff warm air onto my hands so that I could hold hers.

She shifted a little in her bed and winced.

'Do you need more pain relief?' I asked.

She nodded and licked her lips.

'Let me give you some water first, and then I'll get the nurse.'

I dipped a pink sponge into the cup by her bed and then offered it to her mouth. Her tongue found it and she lifted the fingers of her left hand to indicate more.

'Do you want to try the cup? I could lift you a little higher.'

She nodded again. I pressed the buttons that operated the bed and raised the angle of her head. Knowing that too much would be unbearable I was conservative in my estimation of the angle. I offered the cup and she appeared to drink. Then panic registered in her eyes and I stopped. Her mouth was full, and water dripped down her neck.

'I'm so sorry, Kathleen.' I mopped the overflow and used humour to cover my guilt, 'Good job I'm not a nurse.'

I held a flannel to her cheek as the excess spilt from her mouth. She began to cough. Each cough caused her pain.

'I'm so sorry.'

The coughing ceased and I settled her back down. She managed to exert some pressure on my hand and forgive me with her eyes. She was too weak to smile much these days.

'Don't worry,' her nurse reassured me, later. 'Just stick to the dipping sponge.' She looked at me with sympathy as she explained, 'Kathleen is beginning to lose her ability to swallow. I know it's hard to watch, but it's all about keeping her comfortable now.'

Loss of ability to swallow is typical of the final stages of Alzheimer's, but I no longer knew whether it was age, anaemia or dementia that was winning the battle to claim Kathleen. It no longer mattered. As I bundled myself back into my snow clothes, I tried to make conversation. Her sick bed, her dying had floored me more than Alzheimer's had done. For the first time, I didn't know what to say.

'You used to brave all weathers to get your paper,' I said, in a voice that sounded too loud.

I tried to smile as I spoke, hoped that added warmth would be enough to cover my inadequacy.

'You'd pop on your Russian hat, your suede coat and furry boots and march to the shop.'

'I suppose I must have done,' she smiled and raised her left hand.

I hadn't expected a coherent response. I moved closer to her, squeezed her hand, and placed my head next to hers. Simple, meaningless words, but a real connection. It was to be our final conversation; the only coherent words that Kathleen said to me after that moment in the hospital corridor.

'You are very much loved,' I said, struggling not to cry.

I want to believe that she nodded.

Leaving her was never easy, but Shirley, who had reassured me about the water, also took me to one side as I went to punch in the code to exit.

'She's being well looked after.'

'I know she is. Thank you all so much. She knows how cared for she is here.'

'She does. But that's not why I stopped you.'

There was a pause. She laid her hand on my arm. I struggled to keep my composure.

'You are tired. You are here every day, even traipsing through this snow. Sometimes you need a rest, and sometimes those who are dying need to be able to let go. As much as you might want to be by her side, most people hold on to the threads of life whilst their families are near. You need to trust us to love her when you're not here.'

'I do,' I said, tears falling down my cheeks.

'Then allow yourself to rest.'

I cried as I walked back. The beautiful landscape now seemed bleak and uncompromising. Shirley was right. Years of experience had given her the wisdom to see more clearly than me. I trusted them, but I didn't want Kathleen to die alone. I had prayed so many times that she might be released from her pain and slip away whilst

I was holding her hand. But Shirley made me see such a scenario was more romanticism than reality. They would be there, and that was enough.

It was now early February and three weeks since her accident. Kathleen was holding onto life with a tenacity no one had expected, though why we didn't expect it is the bigger mystery. Kathleen had always been stoic.

I decided to go back to an older pattern. Three times a week, maybe four. I was still writing assignments for university and, clouded though my thinking was, I needed to remember my own life too. It was what Philip had meant when he left, and what Shirley was gently encouraging me to do.

Monday was the first day I didn't go in. And it was almost inevitable that the phone rang in the early hours of Tuesday. It was Philip. He didn't need to speak; I knew that she was gone. Passing the receiver to my husband, tears slid soundlessly down the sides of my face soaking into my pillow. The force of grief surprised me.

I thought I was prepared until I realised that you never can be.

25
Not the End

Kathleen passed away on a cold February night. She had a broken hip, anaemia and Alzheimer's disease. These ailments did not define her and the dementia that she lived with for almost a decade did not remove her from us. If prevailing ideology continues to insist that we are what we remember, then Kathleen is testimony to its opposite.

By the time of the hip fracture she could not remember yesterday or last week. She could not remember if she had eaten or even what it meant to be hungry, but she knew that she was loved. She was generous of heart throughout and deeply grateful to Philip, Mark, Terence, me and the Bluebell staff. She could be cross at injustice and frustrated by her own limitations but, at her core, she didn't disappear.

Living with Alzheimer's is not a choice any of us would make. It slowly robs capacity and capabilities and forces dependency on other people. These are not trivial things. It can steal language and capacity to think. It can create paranoia and restlessness. Anxiety can permeate the edges of everything, and confusion blur all previous certainties. Nothing about the disease is easy. Very little about the disease is welcome.

Kathleen's dependency meant an enforced deep trust with me – an unlooked-for privilege that has imprinted itself on my heart. I wrote, during her final weeks when I was learning how to negotiate the path to her death that I hoped she knew how much I valued her being in my life. That even in Alzheimer's she gave as much to me and my family as we gave to her. Perhaps more. I hope she knew how much I loved her.

I know that she was secure in the fact that she was supremely and completely loved by Jesus. Her life had been punctuated by faith and obedience to God. Challenges such as singleness, loneliness and family tensions were all met in the margins of her bible study notes, in her private prayers and public dedication to church. Kathleen knew that in every trial there is an underpinning joy. That joy is the grace of Jesus that gives all those in trust in Him the promise of eternal life.

I'm pretty certain that she knew I loved her. I'm absolutely certain that she knew she was headed for heaven. My favourite Bible verse is John 14:2, 'My Father's house has many rooms; if that were not so, I would have told you. I am going there to prepare a place for you.' It first comforted me as a child when I experienced the death of my Grandpa. It comforts me now as I imagine Kathleen in her heavenly room in her heavenly home where there are 'no more tears' (Rev. 21:4).

The promise of no more tears, does not mean absence of grief for those of us here on earth. Death is loss, and loss should be grieved. But Kathleen was my friend and we don't a have a protocol for this type of grief. A friend does not arrange the funeral, does not decide the readings or the hymns. A friend is not family and suddenly there is nothing left to do. We underestimate the love we feel for our friends. In the long weeks between Kathleen's death and the funeral, I picked up my life. I went to university; I gave a presentation on memory and dementia, including pictures of my friend. I couldn't look at my fellow students as I spoke, knowing that they had read early versions of this book, knowing that they knew how much I loved Kathleen, knowing that they knew how much the presentation was costing me.

I told myself that I was not family. I told myself I had no right to dwell in sadness or grief. This was their loss, not mine. They had decades to draw on – Philip, Terence and Matthew had never known life without Kathleen. They had the right to mourn.

I was blessed that Philip and his family saw things differently. They sent me copies of the order of service for Kathleen's memorial – was I content with their decisions? Of course I was. The service of celebration of Kathleen's life was to be held at Kathleen's church, at my church. My husband and I had the privilege of being in the small choir we had gathered to sing out Kathleen's favourite hymns. My children and my parents were in the congregation. Jill was there, lead sidesperson, doing her job as Kathleen would have wanted her to do. Bob and Helen who had helped out so much whilst Kathleen had remained in her bungalow were sitting quietly at the back. Phil and Val, who had driven her to church and been woken by many an early morning reason for Kathleen's non-attendance in the early days of her dementia were there too. A parade of people, deeply fond of Kathleen – a legacy to her impact on our lives. I sang out as loud and clear as I could, singing my heart to my friend. Occasionally I faltered, my voice cracking, but mainly I kept on as she would have done. I tried to be as strong as she had always been.

My shared faith with Kathleen's family afforded me another privilege – as well as attending the intimate service at the crematorium, they allowed me to say the prayers at the memorial service. The final act. The last thing I could do for my friend. We all trusted in a God whose second greatest commandment is that we should love one another. They knew I loved Kathleen.

Love does not have borders of blood. There doesn't need to be a genetic connection or experience of a lifetime to shed tears, to have a heavy heart. I grieved in silence for months, trying to find medical reasons for malaise. I wasn't ill – I was simply missing my friend.

Enlightened discussion of dementia implores us to 'see the person first and the dementia second.'[1] In other words, it seeks to keep relationship at the core of our interactions with those we love. It is relationships rather than memory that make us who we are. Just weeks after her death a well-meaning church worker asked me if I wanted to take on another old lady, another member of the congregation who was now housebound. I lacked all capacity to reply. Kathleen was not an old lady on a visiting list. She was my friend, established over two decades and an inherent extension of my family. I could not envisage the idea of *replacing* her, of reducing her to a pastoral tick box. I was too harsh in my reaction; the request was lovingly made and meant, but fundamentally it failed to see the person first. To see the character, the personality, the self of another

---

1. Wilkinson, *The Perspectives of People with Dementia: Research Methods and Motivations*, 30.

person 'implies recognition, respect and trust.'[2] Intuitively, Kathleen and I navigated Alzheimer's so that we could keep her self alive.

Such aspiration is not to belittle the difficulties, grief and heartbreak caused by dementia. Rather it asks those of us with memory to curate for those whose memory is no longer reliable. It asks us to hold on to the core of that person when the periphery becomes unfamiliar. It asks us to trust that the impaired cognitive self is more broken than the experienced feeling self.[3]

Nothing about Alzheimer's and other dementias is easy. The experience I have had with Kathleen is unique – to her and to me – as all experiences of dementia are unique. Kathleen was my friend. Perhaps that made it easier for me to adapt to the constantly changing present, to accommodate Alzheimer's in our lives. Perhaps it was also easier for me to see that living with Alzheimer's brought some relief to Kathleen; she was no longer burdened with responsibility and duty. She learnt new skills, indulging in art and craft because she had time to do so. She learnt to give herself over to the care of others.

The basis of every meaningful act is love. Love persists long after memory is splintered and gone.

Statistics show that one in three of us will live with dementia. With love, we can live well.

---

2. Kitwood, *Dementia Reconsidered Revisited*, 7.
3. Gearing et al., *Mental Health Problems in Old Age*, 133.

Acknowledgements

Kathleen knew I was writing this book and was tickled to think her story might one day become something other people would read. I will be forever grateful to her, for she taught me much about grace in adversity, about honesty and vulnerability, and about persistent, sacrificial friendship. She showed me that trusting God is a daily act of will and one worth doing; that we need to live this life with eternity in mind.

There was much blessing in loving her.

I want to thank Kathleen's family for trusting me to write this. Through Kathleen I gained a lifelong friend in Philip, and I am grateful to him for reading the draft copy of *Memorable Loss* before it was sent into the world.

The Writing MA tutors at the University of Warwick guided me and encouraged me. Andrew Williams shaped my ideas of what narrative non-fiction could look like, and he persuaded me to be brave enough to write about what mattered. Alison Ribeiro de Menezes oversaw a unit on memory which inspired much of my additional research; her reaction to a single chapter of *Memorable Loss* convinced me to take a year off and write the rest. Thanks too, to Maureen Freely who was prepared to give up her time during that year to read early drafts and give sound advice.

Early readers from the non-fiction group gave me invaluable critiques – Frances. Lana, Agatha, Vanwy, Bethany and Miriam.

Dr Jason, my friend for over 30 years, verified the medical content.

Other good friends read my manuscript and encouraged me greatly – Steve Ayers, Liz Kennedy, Kate Higley– thank you.

Wisdom and encouragement received from Mark Meynell enabled me to keep going in the journey to publication. Thank you.

Thanks too, to Colin at Christian Focus, and Helen my editor for guiding me through from manuscript to completed book. Thanks to Celia for the cover illustration, and for patience in tweaking the design. Many others worked behind the scenes to bring this book to fruition, and I am grateful to you all.

Deeply personal thanks need to go to my Mum and Dad, Jo, Margaret, Jayne and Lisa for sharing their own experiences of loving someone living with dementia.

And I want to honour my Gran, Betty and my Great Gran, Maude – watching their journey with dementia meant that I had empathy with Kathleen from the start.

Memorable Loss makes it clear that we all forget more than we remember...if I have forgotten anyone who I should have thanked, then forgive me. I am grateful to anyone in my life who has encouraged me in pursuit of this book or helped me to bring it to publication.

Finally, and most importantly, I want to thank my family.

My husband Bri, for always standing alongside me and being on my team, believing in me more than I believe in myself.

My children Emily and James – who read and re-read various incarnations of *Memorable Loss*, and encouraged me unstintingly. And to Emily's husband Jake for spurring me on. All four of these wonderful people shared my graduation day in January 2020, all proud of me for starting the journey that was to end in this book. Since then, Alice has joined the family and is equally excited to see this book become a reality.

Bri, Em and James have been my biggest supporters. I cannot put into words what their love and belief mean to me. I am so blessed to have such skilful editors, proof-readers and cheerleaders.

We live this life only once. To love one another through it, is a gift. In Matthew 22, Jesus said, 'Love the Lord your God with all your heart and with all your soul and with all your mind. This is the first and greatest commandment. And the second is like it: 'Love your neighbour as yourself.'

Thank you for reading *Memorable Loss*. I pray it will be a blessing to you.

Bibliographic References

'1 Guidance | Donepezil, Galantamine, Rivastigmine and Memantine for the Treatment of Alzheimer's Disease | Guidance.' NICE. Accessed August 19, 2019. https://www.nice.org.uk/guidance/ta217/chapter/1-Guidance.

'All in the Mind – Tackling Mental Health Myths,' BBC Sounds. Accessed November 22, 2019. https://www.bbc.co.uk/sounds/play/m000bfj1.

Alzheimer's Society. 'Alzheimer's Society's View on Decision Making.' Accessed September 24, 2019. https://www.alzheimers.org.uk/about-us/policy-and-influencing/what-we-think/decision-making.

Alzheimer's Society. 'Blue Badge Scheme Extended to People with Hidden Disabilities Including People with Dementia.' Accessed September 20, 2019. https://www.alzheimers.org.uk/news/2019-08-30/blue-badge-scheme-extended-people-hidden-disabilities-including-people-dementia-30.

Alzheimer's Society. 'Facts for the Media.' Accessed December 9, 2019. https://www.alzheimers.org.uk/about-us/news-and-media/facts-media.

Alzheimer's Society. 'Over Half of People Fear Dementia Diagnosis, 62 per Cent Think It Means "Life Is Over."' Accessed September 16, 2019. https://www.alzheimers.org.uk/news/2018-05-29/over-half-people-fear-dementia-diagnosis-62-cent-think-it-means-life-over.

Anthony, Andrew. 'Philosophically Speaking, We Can Never Fully Trust Our Memory.' *The Observer*, November 18, 2018, sec. Science. https://www.theguardian.com/science/2018/nov/18/philisophically-speak-we-can-never-fully-trust-our-memory-ylva-hilde-ostby-adventure-in-memory.

Aristotle on Memory and Recollection: Text, Translation, Interpretation, and Reception in Western Scholasticism. BRILL, 2007.

Attix, Deborah K., and Kathleen A. Welsh-Bohmer. *Geriatric Neuropsychology: Assessment and Intervention.* Guilford Publications, 2013.

Baird, Amee, and Séverine Samson. 'Memory for Music in Alzheimer's Disease: Unforgettable?' *Neuropsychology Review* 19, no. 1 (March 2009): 85–101. https://doi.org/10.1007/s11065-009-9085-2.

BBC. 'BBC Radio 4 – The Long and Short of Life Expectancy.' Accessed September 20, 2019. https://www.bbc.co.uk/programmes/m00088mh.

Borges, Jorge Luis. *In Praise of Darkness.* Dutton, 1974.

Bozoki, Andrea C., Hyonggin An, Eva S. Bozoki, and Roderick J. Little. 'The Existence of Cognitive Plateaus in Alzheimer's Disease.' *Alzheimer's & Dementia* 5, no. 6 (November 2009): 470–78. https://doi.org/10.1016/j.jalz.2009.05.669.

CNN, Maddie Bender. 'A Photographic Treatment for Dementia.' CNN. Accessed October 8, 2019. https://www.cnn.com/2018/08/20/health/photographic-treatment-dementia-photos/index.html.

Collins, Jason. GP interview, n.d.

Comas-Herrera, Adelina, and Martin Knapp. 'Cognitive Stimulation Therapy (CST): Summary of Evidence on Cost-Effectiveness,' n.d., 5.

Connerton, Paul. *The Spirit of Mourning: History, Memory and the Body.* Cambridge University Press, 2011.

Cruz, Gilbert. 'Author Carlos Ruiz Zafón.' *Time*, June 30, 2009. http://content.time.com/time/arts/article/0,8599,1907807,00.html.

Daniel A Dombeck, Christopher D Harvey, Lin Tian, Loren L Looger, and David W Tank. 'Functional Imaging of Hippocampal Place Cells at Cellular Resolution during Virtual Navigation.' *Nature Neuroscience* 13, no. 11 (2010): 1433–14340. https://doi.org/10.1038/nn.2648.

Davis, Daniel H.J. 'Dementia: Sociological and Philosophical Constructions.' *Social Science & Medicine* 58, no. 2 (January 2004): 369–78. https://doi.org/10.1016/S0277-9536(03)00202-8.

De Lepeleire, J., J. Heyman, and F. Buntinx. 'The Early Diagnosis of Dementia: Triggers, Early Signs and Luxating Events.' *Family Practice* 15, no. 5 (October 1, 1998): 431–36. https://doi.org/10.1093/fampra/15.5.431.

'Dementia-Short-Guide.Pdf.' Accessed September 16, 2019. http://nuffieldbioethics.org/wp-content/uploads/2014/07/Dementia-short-guide.pdf.

Dementia Statistics Hub. 'Care Services.' Accessed September 30, 2019. https://www.dementiastatistics.org/statistics/care-services/.

Dittrich, Luke. *Patient H.M.: A Story of Memory, Madness and Family Secrets.* Random House, 2016.

Eichenbaum, Howard, Paul Dudchenko, Emma Wood, Matthew Shapiro, and Heikki Tanila. 'The Hippocampus, Memory, and Place Cells: Is It Spatial Memory or a Memory Space?' *Neuron* 23, no. 2 (June 1, 1999): 209–26. https://doi.org/10.1016/S0896-6273(00)80773-4.

Eustache, M.-L., M. Laisney, A. Juskenaite, O. Letortu, H. Platel, F. Eustache, and B. Desgranges. 'Sense of Identity in Advanced Alzheimer's Dementia: A Cognitive Dissociation between Sameness and Selfhood?' *Consciousness and Cognition* 22, no. 4 (December 2013): 1456–67. https://doi.org/10.1016/j.concog.2013.09.009.

Feinstein, Justin S., Melissa C. Duff, and Daniel Tranel. 'Sustained Experience of Emotion after Loss of Memory in Patients with Amnesia.' *Proceedings of the National Academy of Sciences* 107, no. 17 (April 27, 2010): 7674–79. https://doi.org/10.1073/pnas.0914054107.

Ferretti, Louise, Susan M. McCurry, Rebecca Logsdon, Laura Gibbons, and Linda Teri. 'Anxiety and Alzheimer's Disease.' *Journal of Geriatric Psychiatry and Neurology* 14, no. 1 (March 1, 2001): 52–58. https://doi.org/10.1177/089198870101400111.

Foundation, Poetry. 'It Couldn't Be Done by Edgar Albert Guest.' Text/html. Poetry Foundation, October 28, 2019. https://www.poetryfoundation.org/poems/44314/it-couldnt-be-done.

Gearing, Brian, Malcolm Johnson, Tom Heller, and Open University. *Mental Health Problems in Old Age: A Reader.* Wiley, 1988.

Genova, Lisa. *Still Alice*. Simon and Schuster, 2010.

Gerrard, Nicci. *What Dementia Teaches Us About Love*. Penguin UK, 2019.

Graham, Matthew, and Jakki Cowley. *A Practical Guide to the Mental Capacity Act 2005: Putting the Principles of the Act Into Practice*. Jessica Kingsley Publishers, 2015.

Hamann, Stephan. 'Cognitive and Neural Mechanisms of Emotional Memory.' *Trends in Cognitive Sciences* 5, no. 9 (September 1, 2001): 394–400. https://doi.org/10.1016/S1364-6613(00)01707-1.

'History | About Us | University of Exeter.' Accessed October 9, 2019. https://www.exeter.ac.uk/about/facts/history/.

HOPES Huntington's Disease Information. 'About Glutamate Toxicity,' June 26, 2011. https://hopes.stanford.edu/about-glutamate-toxicity/.

'Houston_a_report_2016_final.Pdf.' Accessed October 10, 2019. https://www.ed.ac.uk/files/atoms/files/houston_a_report_2016_final.pdf.

'How Alzheimer's Disease Affects Vision and Perception – VisionAware.' Accessed October 9, 2019. https://www.visionaware.org/info/for-seniors/health-and-aging/vision-loss-and-the-challenges-of-aging/alzheimer%27s-disease/how-alzheimer%E2%80%99s-disease-affects-vision-and-perception/12345.

'How People with Dementia and Their Families Decide about Moving to a Care Home and Support Their Needs: Development of a Decision Aid, a Qualitative Study | BMC Geriatrics | Full Text.' Accessed October 1, 2019. https://bmcgeriatr.biomedcentral.com/articles/10.1186/s12877-016-0242-1.

Karger, Cornelia R. 'Emotional Experience in Patients with Advanced Alzheimer's Disease from the Perspective of Families, Professional Caregivers, Physicians, and Scientists.' *Aging & Mental Health* 22, no. 3 (March 4, 2018): 316–22. https://doi.org/10.1080/13607863.2016.1261797.

King, Stephen. *Duma Key*. Simon and Schuster, 2008.

KITWOOD. *Dementia Reconsidered Revisited: The Person Still Comes First*. McGraw-Hill Education, 2019.

Klíma, Ivan, and Paul R. Wilson. *The Spirit of Prague: And Other Essays*. Granta Books, 1994.

Larrabee, Glenn J. *Forensic Neuropsychology: A Scientific Approach*. Oxford University Press, USA, 2011.

Lindeman, Meghan I. H., Bettina Zengel, and John J. Skowronski. 'An Exploration of the Relationship among Valence, Fading Affect, Rehearsal Frequency, and Memory Vividness for Past Personal Events.' *Memory* 25, no. 6 (July 3, 2017): 724–35. https://doi.org/10.1080/09658211.2016.1210172.

LS Interview. Interview by Karen Martin, October 17, 2018.

Marczinski, Cecile A., and Andrew Kertesz. 'Category and Letter Fluency in Semantic Dementia, Primary Progressive Aphasia, and Alzheimer's Disease.' *Brain and Language* 97, no. 3 (June 1, 2006): 258–65. https://doi.org/10.1016/j.bandl.2005.11.001.

Martin, Karen. EF interview, March 4, 2019.

Martin, Karen. MH interview, October 24, 2019.

Memory and Aging Center. 'Speech & Language.' Accessed October 21, 2019. https://memory.ucsf.edu/symptoms/speech-language.

'Memory Storage – Memory Processes – The Human Memory.' Accessed September 18, 2019. http://www.human-memory.net/processes_storage.html.

Mitchell, Wendy. *Somebody I Used to Know*. Bloomsbury Publishing, 2019.

MIT News. 'The Rise and Fall of Cognitive Skills.' Accessed August 23, 2019. http://news.mit.edu/2015/brain-peaks-at-different-ages-0306.

Moe, Karen E., Michael V. Vitiello, Lawrence H. Larsen, and Patricia N. Prinz. 'Sleep/Wake Patterns In Alzheimer's Disease: Relationships with Cognition and Function.' *Journal of Sleep Research* 4, no. 1 (March 1, 1995): 15–20. https://doi.org/10.1111/j.1365-2869.1995.tb00145.x.

Moran, Tim P. 'Anxiety and Working Memory Capacity: A Meta-Analysis and Narrative Review.' *Psychological Bulletin* 142, no. 8 (August 2016): 831–64. https://doi.org/10.1037/bul0000051.

Mortimer, James A., Amy R. Borenstein, Karen M. Gosche, and David A. Snowdon. 'Very Early Detection of Alzheimer Neuropathology and the Role of Brain Reserve in Modifying Its Clinical Expression.' *Journal of Geriatric Psychiatry and Neurology* 18, no. 4 (December 2005): 218–23. https://doi.org/10.1177/0891988705281869.

National Institute on Aging. 'Social Isolation, Loneliness in Older People Pose Health Risks.' Accessed September 20, 2019. https://www.nia.nih.gov/news/social-isolation-loneliness-older-people-pose-health-risks.

Nilsson, Lars-Göran, and Nobuo Ohta. *Dementia and Memory*. Psychology Press, 2013.

Ólafsdóttir, H. Freyja, Daniel Bush, and Caswell Barry. 'The Role of Hippocampal Replay in Memory and Planning.' *Current Biology* 28, no. 1 (January 8, 2018): R37–50. https://doi.org/10.1016/j.cub.2017.10.073.

Østby, Hilde, and Ylva Østby. *Adventures in Memory: The Science and Secrets of Remembering and Forgetting*. Greystone Books Ltd, 2018.

Panula, Jorma, Harri Pihlajamäki, Ville M Mattila, Pekka Jaatinen, Tero Vahlberg, Pertti Aarnio, and Sirkka-Liisa Kivelä. 'Mortality and Cause of Death in Hip Fracture Patients Aged 65 or Older – a Population-Based Study.' *BMC Musculoskeletal Disorders* 12 (May 20, 2011): 105. https://doi.org/10.1186/1471-2474-12-105.

Peel, Elizabeth. '"The Living Death of Alzheimer's" versus "Take a Walk to Keep Dementia at Bay": Representations of Dementia in Print Media and Carer Discourse.' *Sociology of Health & Illness* 36, no. 6 (2014): 885–901. https://doi.org/10.1111/1467-9566.12122.

Peters, R. 'Ageing and the Brain.' *Postgraduate Medical Journal* 82, no. 964 (February 1, 2006): 84–88. https://doi.org/10.1136/pgmj.2005.036665.

Photographic Treatment. 'About Us.' Accessed October 8, 2019. http://photographictreatment.com/en/about-us/.

'Police at War: Second World War.' Accessed October 18, 2019. http://www.open.ac.uk/Arts/history-from-police-archives/Pol-Cit/polww2.html.

Poulin, Stéphane P., Rebecca Dautoff, John C. Morris, Lisa Feldman Barrett, and Bradford C. Dickerson. 'Amygdala Atrophy Is Prominent in Early Alzheimer's Disease and Relates to Symptom Severity.' *Psychiatry Research* 194, no. 1 (October 31, 2011): 7–13. https://doi.org/10.1016/j.pscychresns.2011.06.014.

Radak, Zsolt, Nicoletta Hart, Linda Sarga, Erica Koltai, Mustafa Atalay, Hideki Ohno, and Istvan Boldogh. 'Exercise Plays a Preventative Role in Alzheimer's Disease.' *Journal of Alzheimer's Disease: JAD* 20 (2010): 777–83. https://doi.org/10.3233/JAD-2010-091531.

Roche, Richard AP, Sinéad L Mullally, Jonathan P McNulty, Judy

Hayden, Paul Brennan, Colin P Doherty, Mary Fitzsimons, et al. 'Prolonged Rote Learning Produces Delayed Memory Facilitation and Metabolic Changes in the Hippocampus of the Ageing Human Brain.' *BMC Neuroscience* 10 (November 20, 2009): 136. https://doi.org/10.1186/1471-2202-10-136.

Rodeheaver, Dean, and Nancy Datan. 'The Challenge of Double Jeopardy.' *American Psychologist*, 1988, 7.

Rose, Frank. 'The Art of Immersion: Why Do We Tell Stories?' *Wired*, March 8, 2011. https://www.wired.com/2011/03/why-do-we-tell-stories/.

Schacter, Daniel L., Donna Rose Addis, and Randy L. Buckner. 'Remembering the Past to Imagine the Future: The Prospective Brain.' *Nature Reviews Neuroscience* 8, no. 9 (September 2007): 657–61. https://doi.org/10.1038/nrn2213.

Schiffrin, Deborah, Anna De Fina, and Anastasia Nylund. *Telling Stories: Language, Narrative, and Social Life.* Georgetown University Press, 2010.

Schliebs, Reinhard, and Thomas Arendt. 'The Cholinergic System in Aging and Neuronal Degeneration.' *Behavioural Brain Research*, The cholinergic system and brain function, 221, no. 2 (August 10, 2011): 555–63. https://doi.org/10.1016/j.bbr.2010.11.058.

Segal, Daniel L., Sara Honn Qualls, and Michael A. Smyer. *Aging and Mental Health.* John Wiley & Sons, 2018.

'Sensory Integration Dysfunction in People with Dementia and People with Autism.' n.d.

'Short and Long Term Memory | HowStuffWorks.' Accessed September 16, 2019. https://science.howstuffworks.com/life/inside-the-mind/human-brain/human-memory2.htm.

Stern, Yaakov. 'Cognitive Reserve in Ageing and Alzheimer's Disease.' *The Lancet. Neurology* 11, no. 11 (November 2012): 1006–12. https://doi.org/10.1016/S1474-4422(12)70191-6.

Suddendorf, Thomas, and Michael C. Corballis. 'The Evolution of Foresight: What Is Mental Time Travel, and Is It Unique to Humans?' *Behavioral and Brain Sciences* 30, no. 3 (June 2007): 299–313. https://doi.org/10.1017/S0140525X07001975.

Taylor, Kathleen Eleanor. *The Fragile Brain: The Strange, Hopeful Science of Dementia.* Oxford University Press, 2016.

'THE BRAIN FROM TOP TO BOTTOM.' Accessed September 26, 2019. https://thebrain.mcgill.ca/flash/i/i_01/i_01_m/i_01_m_ana/i_01_m_ana.html.

The Human Memory. 'Memory Encoding | Memory Processes Storage & Retrieval,' September 25, 2019. https://human-memory. net/memory-encoding/.

Waldemar, Gunhild, and Alistair Burns. *Alzheimer's Disease*. Oxford University Press, 2017.

Wattis, John P, and Stephen Curran. *Practical Psychiatry of Old Age*. 5th ed. Oxford: Radcliffe Publishing, 2013.

'What Happens When You Lose Neurons? | A Moment of Science – Indiana Public Media.' Accessed September 17, 2019. https:// indianapublicmedia.org/amomentofscience/lose-neurons/.

Wilkinson, Heather. 'The Perspectives of People with Dementia: Research Methods and Motivations – Google Books,' 2002. https://books.google.co.uk/books?id=ro-zw8mAjYAC&print sec=frontcover&dq=the+perspectives+of+people+with+deme ntia:+research+methods+and+motivations&hl=en&sa=X&ve d=0ahUKEwjej7f_o5HkAhXEGewKHdh9BPgQ6AEIKjA A#v=onepage&q=the%20perspectives%20of%20people%20 with%20dementia%3A%20research%20methods%20and%20 motivations&f=false.

Williamson, Toby. *Older People's Mental Health Today: A Handbook*. OLM-Pavilion, 2009.

Wilson, R., D. Gilley, D. Bennett, L. Beckett, and D. Evans. 'Hallucinations, Delusions, and Cognitive Decline in Alzheimer's Disease.' *Journal of Neurology, Neurosurgery, and Psychiatry* 69, no. 2 (August 2000): 172–77. https://doi.org/10.1136/jnnp.69.2.172.

Wong, J.G., I.C.H. Clare, A.J. Holland, P.C. Watson, and M. Gunn. 'The Capacity of People with a "mental Disability" to Make a Health Care Decision.' *Psychological Medicine* 30, no. 2 (March 2000): 295–306.

Woods, Robert T, ed. *Psychological Problems of Ageing – Assessment, Treatment and Care.*, n.d.

Christian Focus Publications

Our mission statement –

STAYING FAITHFUL

In dependence upon God we seek to impact the world through literature faithful to His infallible Word, the Bible. Our aim is to ensure that the Lord Jesus Christ is presented as the only hope to obtain forgiveness of sin, live a useful life and look forward to heaven with Him.

Our books are published in four imprints:

CHRISTIAN
FOCUS

Popular works including biographies, commentaries, basic doctrine and Christian living.

CHRISTIAN
HERITAGE

Books representing some of the best material from the rich heritage of the church.

MENTOR

Books written at a level suitable for Bible College and seminary students, pastors, and other serious readers. The imprint includes commentaries, doctrinal studies, examination of current issues and church history.

CF4•K

Children's books for quality Bible teaching and for all age groups: Sunday school curriculum, puzzle and activity books; personal and family devotional titles, biographies and inspirational stories – because you are never too young to know Jesus!

Christian Focus Publications Ltd,
Geanies House, Fearn, Ross-shire,
IV20 1TW, Scotland, United Kingdom.
www.christianfocus.com